Hot and Cold

By Allan Fowler

Consultants

Robert L. Hillerich, Professor Emeritus,
Bowling Green State University, Bowling Green, Ohio;
Consultant, Pinellas County Schools, Florida

Lynne Kepler, Educational Consultant

Fay Robinson, Child Development Specialist

CHILDRENS PRESS®

CHICAGO

GREEN LAKE PUBLIC SCHOOL

Design by Beth Herman Design Associates
Photo Research by Feldman & Associates, Inc.

Library of Congress Cataloging-in-Publication Data

Fowler, Allan.
    Hot and cold / by Allan Fowler.
       p. cm. –(Rookie read-about science)
    ISBN 0-516-06021-X
    1. Heat–Juvenile literature. 2. Cold–Juvenile literature.
    3. Temperature–Juvenile literature. [1. Heat. 2. Cold. 3. Temperature.]
    I. Title. II. Series.
QC256.F68 1994
536–dc20
                                       93-38588
                                         CIP
                                          AC

How hot is a hot day?

3

If you're sweating, it must
be pretty hot.

A swim in cold water will
cool you off.

How cold is a cold day?
If you're shivering, it must
be pretty cold.

Sitting in front of a
fireplace will warm
you up.

To say exactly how hot or cold the weather is, we use a number. This number is called the temperature.

On a warm day, the number is higher than on a cold day. You can find out the temperature by looking at a thermometer.

It feels good to stand in
the warm sun on a bright
spring day.

Most of our heat comes from the sun. Without heat from the sun, few things could grow; few things could live.

Around the North Pole
and South Pole, it is cold
all the time.

Very few kinds of plants
or animals can live where
there is so little heat.

Other places stay warm
all year around.

These places are called the tropics. They are often covered by plants and are filled with animal life.

We put heat to work for us.
We cook our food with heat.

We keep our homes
warm on cold days.

A high, or warm, temperature causes many things to expand, or grow bigger.

On bridges, a little space is left between the steel beams. This gives the beams room to expand on hot days.

19

Hot and cold temperatures can change the form of things. Hard metals will melt in the heat of a fire.

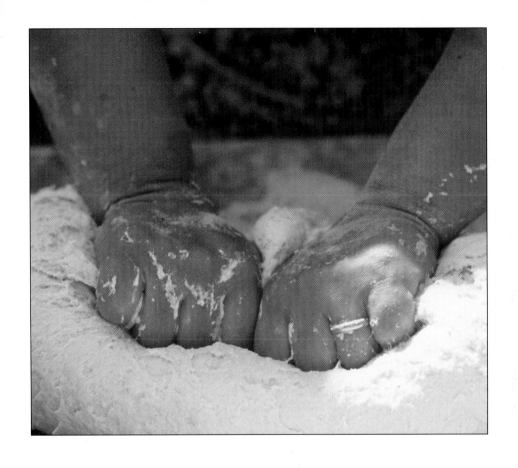

This soft dough becomes a
firm loaf of bread when
you bake it in a hot oven.

If you make water hot
enough, it starts to boil
and turns into steam.

When water drops to a
low enough temperature,
it freezes into ice.

A low, or cold, temperature causes many things to contract, or get smaller.

In the winter, the mercury in a thermometer contracts and shows a low temperature.

25

Although cold makes most things contract, some liquids expand when they freeze.

This milk expanded when it froze — and popped right out of the bottle.

27

28

A mixture of cream, milk, sugar, and flavoring becomes ice cream if it is left in a freezer.

On a warm day, you have to eat your ice cream fast. If you don't, it will melt . . . and then you will be drinking ice cream soup!

Words You Know

sweating

shivering

boil   steam

tropics

temperature   thermometer

heat

ice

Index

About the Author

Allan Fowler is a free-lance writer with a background in advertising. Born in New York, he lives in Chicago now and enjoys traveling.

Photo Credits

PhotoEdit – ©David Young-Wolff, 4, 16, 17, 30 (top left); ©Merritt A. Vincent, 7; ©Tony Freeman, 8, 11, 22, 30 (bottom left), 31 (top); ©Mark Burnett, 19

Tom Stack & Associates—©David M. Dennis, 19 (inset)

SuperStock International, Inc. – Ron Dahlquist, Cover; ©James Ong, 5; ©Tom Rosenthal, 10, 25; ©Peter Van Rhijn, 14, 30 (bottom right); ©Prim and Ray Manley, 20, 31 (bottom left); ©George Jacobs, 23, 31 (bottom right)

Tony Stone Images— ©Ken Griffiths, 12; ©Bryn Campbell, 13

Valan – ©Robert C. Simpson, 6, 30 (top right); ©John Cancalosi, 15; ©Kennon Cooke, 21; ©A.B. Joyce, 27; ©V. Wilkinson, 28

COVER: Girls eating ice cream

Marisol

by Gary Soto

American Girl

To Idalia, Patricia, Sandra, and Gina,
the best darn teachers of Hebbronville, Texas

Published by Pleasant Company Publications
Copyright © 2005 by American Girl, LLC
Printed in China.
07 08 09 10 C&C 10

Visit our Web site at **americangirl.com**.

The characters and events portrayed in this book are fictitious. Any similarity to real persons, living or dead, is coincidental and not intended by the author.

Illustrations by Richard Jones

Picture credits: p. 139—Photo by Jamie Young; p. 140—Courtesy of Cynthia Betz; p. 141—Will Capellaro.

Cataloging-in-Publication Data available from the Library of Congress.

Contents

1

Saturday Morning

On Saturdays, I like to spend the whole morning in my bedroom. It faces Harrison Park, and I can sit on my trunk by the window and take in the action at the park and on the street below. In my trunk I keep my clothes all nice and tidy . . . well, at least my dance things. No promises about the rest! Today I watched my friend Victor sucking a grape-flavored *raspada* while he kicked a soccer ball back and forth off a garage door.

There was Mr. Mendoza, our upstairs neighbor, swinging his briefcase. Is he a businessman with a brief-case full of important papers? No, he's a nice old man with a briefcase filled with dominos. He plays dominos with his friends six days a week at the Senior Citizens

Center. The rest of the time he chugs about in the apartment above ours in slippers—he is mouse quiet. It appeared that he was a winner this morning—he was coming home whistling "*Cielito Lindo*."

I leaned part of the way out of the window and waved to Mr. Mendoza. He raised his eyes upward and waved a hand the color of rusty sycamore leaves—the color they are when they fall and tumble in autumn.

Am I a nosy neighbor? No, I am Marisol Luna, first and only daughter of Hector and Elisa Luna. They are my parents and the loves of my life.

Well, kind of. I also love dancing. I was born to dance—even in the crib. According to Mom, when I was six months old I could shake my rattle like a *maraca*. By nine months, I was standing and moving back and forth in a cha-cha-cha. Later, when I was two years old, I danced standing on my father's shoes. My father is my first and only boyfriend, even though he has eyes for another woman—Mom!

I love my parents. I love our apartment. And I love

my bedroom. It has a ceiling full of stars that glow in the dark and make me believe that I live on my own planet. But it wasn't dark right then. No, it was Saturday morning and I was only half-dressed—I had my socks on, the ones I would wear all day, and my nightgown, which I would pull over my head when it was time to leave for dance class.

You see, my bedroom is also my dance studio. This morning I was practicing a ballet *folklórico* step that my Mexican folk dance troupe had been working on. It's an uncomplicated pattern of one foot over the other, then two steps back. It's part of the *Jarabe Tapatío,* a dance that we learned months ago and would be performing in just a few days. Other times I practice my *pliés* and *jetés* for my other ballet class. I haven't really done any jazz since I took a class last summer. Sometimes I like to wear the feather boas I got at jazz class around the house. I feel like a bird in a beautifully feathered nest.

What I practice depends on which dance class I have—and my mood, of course. Ballet folklórico is happy dancing, and traditional ballet is more graceful and exact—*Mademoiselle* Juliette is strict about posture.

My cat, Rascal, came in prancing. Lovingly, he poked his nose at my shin. He expected me to rub his belly and scratch behind his ears. I bent down and petted him, but not a lot, because Rascal was in trouble with me.

"Where were you last night?" I asked. I tried to roar a scold, but how could I? I love my cat, who arrived as a kitten in the rain three years ago, when I was only seven years old.

Some nights Rascal sleeps inside, curled into my covers. Other nights he walks the rickety fences of our neighborhood. And moon or no moon, Rascal meows his silly head off.

Rascal meowed now. I picked him up and tossed him softly onto my bed. He stretched his princely limbs and then curled up. He is so lazy, even though he's a young cat with spring in his legs. He blinked his eyes twice and fell asleep while I continued practicing. I was partway through the routine again when I heard my father calling from another part of our apartment.

"*Mi'jita,*" he yelled. There was panic in his voice.

I went running and found him in the kitchen with his left eye squinted shut.

"What's wrong?" I asked. He was holding a kitchen knife and, for a moment, I thought that he had cut himself.

He told me in Spanish that he had gotten chili in his eye, the one that was closed. I sized up what my *papi* had been doing while Mom was gone—making *salsa.* He had been cutting *jalapeño* chilies and mashing them in the *molcajete,* the stone grinding bowl we had gotten in Mexico.

Obviously, my otherwise smart dad had rubbed his face. The chili juice must have found its way into his eyes, which are the handsomest thing about him. That's a family joke. Dad is a great guy, but, well, he's no movie star.

"Wet a paper towel," he pleaded.

"First, put down that knife."

He placed the knife on the counter and then sat down at the table.

I dampened a paper towel under the kitchen faucet and dabbed at Dad's eye until he blinked and proclaimed, "*Mejor!* Better. I'm healed! I can see!"

"Let *me* see," I said, unconvinced.

He leaned over and showed me his eye.

"Can you see?" I asked. His eye was as red as the tomatoes in his salsa.

He rotated his eye, the big joker, and exclaimed, "Yes, I can see you." He stood up, washed his hands under the faucet, and picked up the knife again. He started cutting a softball-sized onion.

"What have you been doing?" he asked as he chopped.

"Practicing," I answered.

Dad knew that there was a dance performance at the Senior Citizens Center on Thursday. He glanced at the calendar on the refrigerator. The magnets that held the calendar had lost their power, so the calendar had slid down, way down. If Rascal were smart enough, he could easily have read that today was October 22.

If he were even smarter, he would have known that Halloween was just over a week away.

"You're going to be at the performance—right?" I asked Dad.

"*Claro qué sí,*" he sang. But then he scrunched up his face as if he were thinking, *Or will I?* You see, my dad works for the city. His job? He maintains the trains that roll and clang through our city of Chicago. He is an electrician with his own truck, and he has two guys who ride with him. They keep the power going for the trains.

My face fell. "You mean you might miss my performance?"

He shrugged his shoulders. "I don't know, *mi'ja.* Maybe I'm going to have a long day." His face was flat, without emotion, but then a smile quivered at the corners of his mouth. "Of course I won't miss it. I'll be there." He then asked if I was hungry.

I stared at the mountain of salsa in a plastic bowl. He would soon snap on a lid to keep its mighty fumes in.

"Where's Mom?" I asked. I mean, my papi is a good

cook, but Mom is an artist in the kitchen.

"What? You don't trust me?" He slid the knife blade covered with chopped onions into his salsa.

"Not in the kitchen!" I said. "Look at what you did to your eye."

He rolled his eyes and asked me to get the eggs out of the refrigerator.

"OK," I said. I was willing to give him a chance.

He asked for the black frying pan.

"The small one or the big one?" I was reaching into the dark cavern of the oven drawer where we keep the pots and pans.

"*La cacerolita*," he sang. "The little one." He took the black pan I handed him and buttered it.

Breakfast, I thought. Dad's idea of breakfast is a single lightly salted egg and a *tortilla* heated up on the back burner. He held up the egg and was ready to crack it on the edge of the pan when, presto! Mom came in with a bag of groceries heavy in her arms.

"What tragedy is about to happen here?" Mom

asked. She put the groceries down on the counter. She patted Dad's shoulder and said, "*A ver.* Let's see."

Mom and I listened as Dad described a perfect sunny-side-up egg. But when he cracked the egg and let it slip into the pan, the yolk began to spread.

Neither Mom nor I said anything until Dad grumbled, then asked, "You like scrambled, don't you?"

And that's what we had—scrambled eggs with little bits of weenie, plus potatoes and tortillas and Dad's spicy salsa. We ate at the crowded kitchen table. I didn't even complain about Dad hogging the space. He was reading the sports section, and every time he turned the page, the newspaper raked across my potatoes.

Finally, Dad put the newspaper down. Rubbing his chin, he seemed to be reflecting on some large question about life. "You know, these tomatoes in *la salsa,* they don't have much flavor. We need to grow our own tomatoes."

"But you need a yard to grow your own." Mom waved a fork at the window over the sink. "And we have no yard."

"Sounds like we might need our own house," Dad said to Mom. Then his eyes slid over to me. I used a bit of tortilla to scoop up the last of my egg, and I popped it all into my mouth.

"Mmmm, that was good, Dad," I said.

"It would be even better, mi'ja, if we could grow our own chilies and tomatoes."

My parents looked at me, and looked and looked. They were up to something.

Mom is only five foot three, but she is the captain of our van, which she maneuvered over potholes on the way to dance class.

Mom gazed up into the rearview mirror. "How's your mom?" she asked my friend Sara, who is also a member of my ballet folklórico troupe. Sara's mother had hurt her back playing soccer.

"She's OK," Sara answered. "She's surfing right now."

My mom's eyes doubled in size in the rearview mirror.

"Surfing! In Chicago?"

Sara giggled into her sleeve. "I mean *sewing*. She's *sewing* my new dance skirts."

I laughed, too. I goof up my words all the time for no good reason. I'll say, "Mom, there's a can on the telephone and he wants to walk with you," when I mean to say "man" and "talk." What can I say, except my mind goes one way and my mouth another.

"It's so crowded here on the weekend," Mom remarked as she craned her neck in search of a parking space.

We circled the block twice, even though I had hollered, "Mom, right here!" I had spotted a parking space, but she missed it—and the next one, too. In Chicago, parking spaces in front of schools on Saturday mornings are difficult to find because of all the soccer games. Finally Mom pulled into a space, and we were out of the van and running to class before she'd even turned off the engine. We were exactly five minutes late.

"Don't rush, ladies," I heard a voice call.

When I turned, I spotted *Maestra* Davila, our dance teacher, juggling a lot of things in her arms. She was behind us, so she was five minutes and a few seconds late.

"Great parking," she said to my mom, who caught up to us while talking on her cell phone. Mom smiled and waved, her fingers working like she was playing the piano.

"I'll be there in a sec," Mom said.

We continued walking, our dance teacher in the center and Mom, on the phone, trailing behind.

"Let me help," Sara said. She took a bundle of dance clothes from our teacher's arms. But the funny thing was that then Sara leaned around Maestra Davila and handed me *her* stuff to carry.

I felt a tap on my shoulder. I turned. It was Jesse, one of the other dancers.

"Let me help you," he said and took the stuff from my arms.

Jesse is sometimes my partner and sometimes Sara's partner. Other times he is no one's partner because, well, he's nice and everything, but he just can't dance. But his mom wants him to take dance lessons, so he has to. He gets by OK in ballet folklórico, but I can't imagine him in jazz or my other ballet class. Mademoiselle Juliette might lose her sweet patience.

"Don't forget about Thursday," Maestra Davila said, pulling open the front door of our elementary school. "We'll meet in front of the Senior Citizens Center."

"Yeah," I answered for Sara and Jesse. Our footsteps clicked down the empty hallway.

"On Thursday," Maestra Davila said in mock anger, "there'll be no tardiness . . . especially from your teacher!"

We nodded with great seriousness as we stepped through another door and headed to class in the school gymnasium. We followed the tinkling Veracruz harp music that echoed off the walls. As we got closer, our feet started skipping to its happy rhythm.

2

Something's Up

I ran up the steps to our apartment, nearly blinded because my puffy folklórico skirts were gathered in my arms like a dance partner. I couldn't see over them. I kicked the bottom of the door twice, our secret signal to open up.

"Dad!" I called. "Papi! Hurry up!"

He opened up the door. He was wearing the Chicago Cubs baseball jersey I had given him for his birthday years and years ago. His right hand was gripping a paintbrush thick with white paint.

As I hurried past him, he bowed like a butler. I set my skirts down on the couch.

"What are you doing?" I asked.

He pointed to the kitchen with the paintbrush. "Painting."

Mom followed me in, her cell phone pressed to her ear. Mom is an accountant with lots of math figures inside her head. Now she hung up and flapped her cell phone closed like a mousetrap.

"Hi," Mom greeted Dad, who gave her a quick smile, then collapsed the smile and swiveled his eyes toward me.

Something is up, I thought. I stood between my parents with my hands on my hips.

"Did you tell her?" Dad asked.

Tell me what? I crossed my arms across my chest.

Mom shook her head, stirring her earrings, which jangled like wind chimes.

Dad munched his lower lip and sighed. He stared at the ceiling, through which we heard Mr. Mendoza's chair creak loudly. In the silence of our apartment, we could hear that his TV was tuned to a Spanish-language program.

"We're moving," Dad announced finally.

For a second I thought he had said "mooing," but I

couldn't recall ever "mooing." Then the word struck me. Dad had said "moving," as in *moving away*—as in losing my friends, my school, my neighborhood, my height chart on my bedroom door frame!

"You're kidding!" I said in disbelief, flapping my arms at my sides like a penguin. I noticed that the paintbrush in Dad's hand was beginning to run. Now I understood. Dad was spiffing up the apartment because we were moving.

"Dad and I think it's time that we get out of this neighborhood," Mom said. She explained that it was no place for me to grow up. It was dangerous, and there was no place for me to play.

"I can play in the street," I argued, not too brightly.

"Yeah, and get run over," Mom predicted.

"You'll be safer there," Dad added.

"Where's 'there'?" I asked, and then I continued before Dad could respond. "But it doesn't matter where, since I like it *here*." At that moment, two men outside began yelling at each other. A car door slammed, and we heard the sound of screeching cars echo between the apartment buildings. Then silence.

"See," Mom said, pointing outside.

Sure, it was noisy. And it wasn't a fancy neighborhood like you see on TV. But I had friends on the block. Even the cats—striped ones, black ones, white ones, spotted ones, and the ones that looked like they were wearing tuxedos—were my friends!

"But why?" I demanded. "What about school? My friends? My dance classes?"

Dad escaped to the kitchen and put the paintbrush in the sink. He came back to the living room but seemed in no hurry to tell me why we had to move. His tongue flipped about in his mouth until he finally said, "Because."

I thought Mom would say something, but she didn't.

"Dad!" I screamed. "That's no reason."

But then I stopped, because I knew that I shouldn't be yelling at either of them. They were my parents. What could I do except turn on my heel and go to my bedroom?

I flung open the door and threw my skirts and myself onto my bed. I stared at the stars pasted to the ceiling, pale now.

"I don't want to move!" I cried. I looked up at the shelf, where my stuffed animals sat like judges. They, too, appeared sad. I pictured packing them into a box for their journey to a new house.

I heard footsteps—Mom's—and a rap, like a small bird pecking on my door.

"You want some soup?" Mom asked through the closed door.

"No," I answered. "I'm not hungry."

Mom went away without a word.

But the soup's aroma soon filled the apartment and made my stomach growl. I got up, pressed my hand into my stomach, and went to my trunk by the window. I keep a stash of candies and other stuff under my folded leotards. I chose the "other stuff," which was beef jerky. I tore off a piece and chewed with my mouth open—who cared what I looked like at that moment?

"Hey, Mari!" Through my window I heard a voice calling to me. I peeked out.

It was Victor from down the street. When I raised the window and stuck my head out, he hollered, "We need another girl player for our team."

The boys were playing basketball in the street. The hoop is a rim from a bicycle wheel that Dad had nailed to the telephone pole.

"I can't play right now," I said. "Why don't you get Becky?"

"Becky's in trouble. Her mom won't let her out of the house 'cause she used the blender to mix some cement."

Mix cement? I was scared to ask.

Victor stood looking up at me. He seemed so small in the street, and he would get even smaller once we moved away. He is one of my best guy friends. He always lets me shoot baskets, even though I'm not really very good.

"Wait a minute!" I hollered. I got up, opened the trunk again, and reached for my stash of candy. I scooped some up in my hands and leaned out the window. "Here!" I yelled. "Catch!" I sent the candy raining down on the street. One of the candies—a jawbreaker—landed right in Victor's outstretched palm.

"Sweet!" he yelled after he unwrapped it and stuck it in his mouth. "It's watermelon—my favorite!"

I didn't say why I was giving my candy away— that we were moving and that Mom and Dad would probably make me get rid of things. No, I just closed the window and stayed there in my bedroom. Even though I wasn't in trouble. Even though I didn't know where we were moving. Or really why.

Instead of wallowing in self-pity, I decided to practice. Dancing always makes me feel better. Besides, I wanted to work on the dance step Maestra Davila had taught—or had tried to teach—us that morning. It is called *El Caimán,* and I had to memorize it. It is a *tap, tap, tap* of the left foot, swing to your left, and *tap, tap, tap* with the right foot and a swing to the right. Then there are a flurry of steps in place and a full circle with your partner, who then pretends to plant a kiss on your cheek—*Asco!* Yuck! I kissed the air just a little peck, like when I kiss my Uncle Julio's shiny cheek.

I was practicing this new dance when I heard what I imagined were dance steps from the apartment above. I stopped, listened. I heard a few more steps, then nothing.

That's weird, I said to myself. I know that Mr. Mendoza doesn't dance—he only shuffles. Plus, he's too old.

I started practicing again. But when I again heard steps from above that echoed my own, I stopped and stared at the ceiling. This time they didn't stop. I sat down on my bed and I listened to the crisp dance steps that carried the rhythm far better than mine had done.

Am I going crazy? I wondered. I shouted at the ceiling, "Mr. Mendoza, is that you?"

There was a long silence and then a *clink* against my window. I hurried to look out the window.

"What?" I asked, as I shoved it open and leaned out.

It was Victor with his basketball team behind him. His mouth was smeared with candy. He cleared his throat and asked, "You got any more, Marisol?"

I pitched out one more handful of candy and watched the boys scramble to catch it all. Then I closed the window and raised my face to the ceiling again. *Who is up there who dances better than I do?*

That afternoon Mom and Dad prodded me into the van for the thirty-minute drive to our new house, which they explained is in Des Plaines. The drive was boring. It was sad, too. They told me that we were going to move next weekend.

"Next weekend? Like in seven days? Like before Halloween?" I asked, shocked by how soon it was. "But—"

"You'll like it," Mom said, flipping through a furniture catalog.

Instead of acting like a big baby, I bit my tongue and counted to ten in Spanish before I said weakly, "Maybe I will." I was upset, but I regretted my earlier tantrum.

"You'll have your own bedroom," Dad said brightly. I sensed that he was about to tell me about the bedroom he had shared with his three brothers, but he held his tongue.

I resisted the urge to shout, *I already have my own bedroom!* I figured that another outburst would only hurt my parents' feelings, and I didn't want to do that. So I looked out the van window and watched the Chicago I knew get smaller and smaller.

Soon we were getting out of the van and crunching through fall leaves in a suburb that even I had to admit was pretty nice. I turned when I heard a dog bark. He was in the next yard and his nose poked between the slats of the fence. He rolled his tongue over his lips and whined to be petted.

"He's so cute," Mom sang.

"Maybe we'll get a dog," Dad said.

"But what about Rascal?" I asked.

My parents agreed that maybe it wasn't wise to have a dog and cat at the same time.

"Well, I guess Rascal has to go," Dad said jokingly.

"Daaad!"

The subject was dropped. I followed my parents up the steps and into the house. I was struck by the high ceiling and the echoes that came off the walls when I said, "It's nice." I wasn't convinced, but I was trying to be agreeable.

"Very nice," Dad agreed, pocketing the house keys.

"I'm going to put the new sofa there," Mom said. She pointed to the area by the front window. I looked out the window and saw someone shuffling down the front steps of another house. He was an elderly man with wings of gray in his hair, and he was holding the handrail. He reminded me of Mr. Mendoza. He was even wearing slippers. I heard the dog from the other yard bark again.

"Come with me," Mom ordered sweetly, putting an arm around my shoulder.

Mom and I bounced up squishy carpeted stairs to the second floor.

"That's our room, and that's the extra bedroom—for guests and for my office," Mom said, pointing out the rooms. She then covered my eyes with her hands—I could smell on her wrists the perfume I had gotten her for her birthday—and led me down the hallway. When she pulled her hands away, I blinked in the bright light.

"And this is your bedroom," she said. "Do you like it?"

I noticed right away that the bedroom was carpeted, and my heart sank. I wondered how I could practice in my room. To do it right, I needed a wooden floor. How could I get ready to perform on a real stage by practicing on carpet? Or maybe my dancing days were over. Was that possible? I realized that Mom hadn't mentioned a dance studio in Des Plaines.

"Yeah, I like it," I lied, trying to sound cheerful. "But . . . it has carpet."

Mom scrunched up her face. She didn't understand because she isn't a dancer.

"Where am I going to practice?"

"Practice?"

"Like dance, Mom."

Mom was going to say something when her cell phone rang. This gave me time to look out the bedroom window, where I plan to spend a lot of time leaning on my elbows looking in the direction of Chicago, which is my *real* home. I would miss my school and friends and all my neighbors. And my dance classes. I would even miss the city noise Mom and Dad complained about. And poor Rascal would miss his cat friends.

From the window, I spied a girl about my age playing with the dog that we had seen earlier. Her sweater sleeves were long and her hands were hidden in them.

The girl looked up, and for a split second I had the dumb thought of ducking from view. The girl waved a hand hidden in the sleeve of her sweater. I waved and formed the word "hi" on my lips, but I turned away when my mom called me: "Mi'ja, *ven!* Come and see!"

I found Mom in my parents' bedroom. She led me into the attached bathroom, where Dad was sitting on the edge of the biggest bathtub in the whole world—or in all the world that I have seen so far in my ten years.

"*Chihuahua!*" I crowed.

I pictured the whole neighborhood getting into the bathtub. I pictured myself sitting with a soda on the edge of the tub. *Ah, what a life!* I thought.

"It has six jets," Dad remarked. He was wearing his funny reading glasses and was studying the owner's manual.

"That's two for each of us," I remarked.

Dad took off his glasses and wiped them as if they were steamed up. "Don't even go there," he warned.

Right then I knew that the tub was off-limits. I pictured all of my friends climbing out of the tub, dripping water as they descended the stairs. The party was over.

3

Who Is She?

When we got home from the new house, it was time for Rascal's monthly flea and tick drops. It's my job to put the drops on the fur at the back of his neck. Mom pointed out that it wouldn't hurt if I brushed him, too. It doesn't hurt him, but he doesn't like it. He somehow knew what was up, because he took off running. I chased Rascal from under tables and chairs, from behind our couch, and finally to the top of the curtains, where he clung for his precious nine lives.

"Come here!" I yelled. "Get off the curtains before Mom gets mad!"

High-flying Rascal dropped like a sack. He scampered from the living room to my bedroom and then into the kitchen, where he skidded to a halt. Food is Rascal's undoing. Foolishly he stopped to sniff the air for the aroma of beans simmering on a low flame. He closed his eyes, and that's when I grabbed him—and daubed the medicine along his back. I also gently combed his fur with the cat brush.

"You're such a baby," I said, scratching his head when I was done. "That didn't even hurt."

Rascal blinked his blue eyes and walked into the living room, where he sat facing the front door.

"OK, you be that way!" I said in fake anger. I opened the door for him, and he left without giving me a single good-bye meow. I stuck my head into the hallway and watched him slip outside through the open hall window.

It was only four thirty. Dad had gone to get the van washed, and Mom was in the kitchen on the phone. And me? I veered into my bedroom and kicked off my shoes. As much as I hated the thought of moving, I was already thinking about packing for the big move. Mom had said she wanted me to get rid of stuff so that she could buy new stuff. *Let's see,* I thought to myself as I surveyed my things. *What has to go?*

Nothing, I answered myself. I was going to take everything, even the door frame with my height markings—if Dad would let me. But he wouldn't, of course. And I knew for sure he wouldn't jackhammer up the cement in the back where I had pressed my handprints when I was four years old.

Suddenly I found myself dancing, my hands gripping the hem of an invisible folklórico skirt. I hummed and turned, picking up the rhythm we'd worked on that morning in class. Then I became aware of rumbling dance steps echoing mine from above.

I stopped. The steps stopped. I looked up at the ceiling. I conjured up an image of Mr. Mendoza holding the hem of an invisible skirt. *No way.* I shook my head until the image disappeared.

"Are you mocking me?" I barked at the ceiling.

Other than a creak, the ceiling said nothing. No voice above me taunted, "Yeah, I'm making fun of you."

I had to have some answers. I stuck my head into the kitchen and told Mom, "I'll be back in a sec."

She mumbled absentmindedly, "Don't be long. We're having *enchiladas* tonight." Mom sometimes doesn't really listen, especially when she's reading a recipe or talking on the phone. And now she was reading a Mexican cookbook.

I walked up one flight and knocked on the door to Mr. Mendoza's apartment. I heard footsteps that didn't sound like Mr. Mendoza's. His footsteps sort of slide, like he is on skis, and these steps were clearer and crisper, but not loud.

I was puzzling over this when the door opened and a woman in a leotard stared out at me. She had black hair that was pulled back into a bun. Her face was red, as if she had been running up the steps. *Who is she?*

"Are you selling something?" the woman asked.

I shook my head.

"Is the radio bothering you?" she asked.

I shook my head.

"Would you like to come in?" the woman asked.

I hesitated.

"Is Mr. Mendoza in?" I asked, and—nosy me—I wondered if he had a girlfriend. I knew that he had been married but that his wife had died before I was born.

"No, he's out playing dominos."

I imagined Mr. Mendoza hunkered over a game at the Senior Citizens Center.

The woman smiled. "I guess he's having fun." Then she introduced herself as Miss Gloria Mendoza, his daughter. She remarked, "I heard you dancing down-stairs." She cast her eyes upward and opened the door a little wider. "You were doing *El Caimán,* weren't you?"

"How did you know?" I asked. I could feel my mouth sag open a little.

"I used to dance folklórico," she explained. "And now—" She looked down at her leotard. "And now I just work out for exercise." Then she giggled with a hand over her mouth. She confessed that she had been teas-ing me a little by repeating my dance steps. "Bad!" she scolded, and playfully spanked her own wrist.

But she was far from "bad." In fact, I thought she was wonderful. Her eyes were beautiful, and her smile was natural and warm.

"I didn't know Mr. Mendoza had a daughter," I remarked, unable to think of anything else to say.

"He does, and that's me." Her eyes shone. She seemed proud to be his daughter. "And you're Marisol, right?"

I nodded, wondering how she knew. Still, when she asked again if I would like to come in, I took a few steps backward and said, "Better not."

"Then I'll come down." She left the door open while she hurried to get a wrap, then pulled on a Chicago Bears sweatshirt instead. She slipped on sandals as she hurried out the door with her house key dangling from a cord on her wrist like a bracelet.

"Let's go," she said.

We walked side by side down the steps, and then I pushed open our front door. "Please come in," I said.

"Mmmm," the woman said as she stepped into our living room. "Something smells good."

Mom was still in the kitchen, and Dad was still out.

"Mom!" I called. "We have a visitor!" I led the way into the kitchen.

Mom stood at the stove, wearing an apron to protect her clothes from the splash of hot oil as she prepared enchiladas. She looked up and, before she spoke to me, greeted our guest with a "Hey, girl." She put down her spatula and gave Gloria Mendoza a quick kiss on each cheek.

"You know . . . Miss Mendoza?" I asked.

"Of course," Mom answered.

"How come I don't know her?"

"I thought you knew everything," Mom said, teasing me. Mom had to bring up the time I had boasted, after getting straight A's, that I knew everything. Well, it was true; I knew everything up to that point—third grade!

"Oh, I'm just teasing," Mom said. "Yes, I know Gloria, Mr. Mendoza's daughter. We met long ago when she came back to visit her father. Now she's living with him."

"That's right. At least for a while," Miss Mendoza said. Then she told me that she was back from New York, where she had been a dancer.

Right then I got dreamy. I mean, New York! A dancer! I pictured myself on a stage, with a spotlight slowly swiveling toward me. The spotlight settled on me, and applause thundered in my ears.

"But how do you know ballet folklórico?" I asked, after the image of my success broke when Mom opened the squeaky oven door.

"That's how I started. Here, in Chicago."

"Really?"

She nodded her head. "When I was about your age," she continued.

I tried to imagine Miss Mendoza being my age, and I had to wonder if she had ever been my height. She was tall, maybe even taller than Dad.

"I took lessons at the playground on Roosevelt

Street. I also took tap and modern, and traditional ballet—any kind of dance class I could." She told us that when she was twenty, she had moved to New York and had danced for the Radio City Rockettes for six years, then danced on Broadway before opening her own dance studio.

"No way," I said, rocking on the heels of my shoes. "A Rockette!"

Miss Mendoza propped her hands on her hips. "You don't believe me?" She had a fake stern look and, behind that look, a smile.

"Yeah, I believe you." And I did. I could see by the way she moved, by the way she *stood*, that she was a dancer. It's just that I hadn't ever met a *real* dancer, someone who had danced in the lights of New York.

"I see you two have a lot to talk about," Mom said. "You can go into the living room and get to know each other. Gloria, would you like to stay for dinner?"

"Claro!"

We went into the living room, where Miss Mendoza

asked me to show her *El Caimán.*

"Very good," she chimed after I demonstrated my steps.

"I've been dancing for about two years," I said proudly. "Mostly ballet folklórico—that's my favorite and how I got started—but now also ballet, and last summer I even did some jazz." I held back a smile, like I had water in my mouth and was getting ready to send it flying—Victor and I did that all the time in summer. "Ballet is the hardest. I still feel stiff, even though my teacher, Mademoiselle Juliette, tries to compliment me."

"Mademoiselle Juliette wants you to keep trying, mi'ja," Miss Mendoza said. "Traditional ballet is hard for everyone, especially at the beginning."

"Was it hard for you, too?" I asked.

She laughed, clapped her hands together, and said, "Claro. But it's worth all the hard work, because it's the foundation for everything else a serious dancer does. You are a serious dancer, yes? Let's see your *pas de chat.*"

I switched gears into ballet mode. Pas de chat means

"cat step," but I've never seen Rascal move like that! After a bit of that, Miss Mendoza asked me to do my folklórico routine again and watched my steps closely.

"Very nice," Miss Mendoza remarked after I finished. "I remember *El Caimán* well, and some others, but not a lot. Do it one more time." She corrected a couple of my steps and then kicked off her sandals to demonstrate.

Miss Mendoza made it look easy. She made me do the steps over and over until I was out of breath.

"Very good, young lady," she said. "You have excellent posture and a subtle rhythm. That will help you in ballet, too. And tap, of course. You'll want to start that soon."

Once again I held back my smile. I couldn't wait to tell Sara about Miss Mendoza!

Miss Mendoza excused herself then, saying that she was going up to dress for dinner and would be back in a few minutes.

Dress for dinner? I wondered. She looked dressed to me. Dad wouldn't have minded the Chicago Bears sweatshirt. The Bears are his favorite football team.

She disappeared before I could put back the rug that I had rolled up like a *burrito*. After I finished unrolling it, I returned to the kitchen and washed my hands so that I could help Mom grate cheese. Then I opened a can of black olives. After I poured off the liquid from the can, I stuck a few olives on the ends of my fingers before I chomped them.

"Mom, she's a real dancer," I stated dreamily.

"I hear she was real good, mi'ja." Mom tapped a large spoon against the black pan where the beans were frying into *refritos*. She added a little milk and three pinches of yellow cheese.

I studied Mom's face to see if she was in a good mood. She was. So I risked asking, "Mom, do we really have to move?"

Now that I had just met Miss Mendoza, I had one *more* reason for not wanting to move.

Mom sighed and said, "Yes, we have to. It's going to be better for you, and for us."

My shoulders sank. I wanted to ask, "What about

my dance classes?" But I held my tongue. I regretted bringing up our move when we should all be happy because we were having a special guest for dinner. I love my mom and didn't want to put her in a bad mood. So instead, I went into the dining room and busied myself setting the table with napkins—the cloth ones—and forks and knives. I put out spoons, too, though I wasn't sure if we were going to need them.

I returned to the kitchen.

"I know it's going to be hard to move," Mom tried to explain. It was still on her mind. "But it's for the best. Our new house will be closer to my work. Maybe I won't have to be on the phone so much when I'm home. Won't *that* be nice?" Mom then cut a look to the cabinet that held the dinner plates—the good ones. I turned to get them out. Mom was going all out for Miss Mendoza!

"Marisol is a natural dancer," Miss Mendoza said at dinner. "She has a beautiful line—perfect for ballet."

I blushed and drank some water to keep from smiling really big.

"She just needs to continue studying," she added. "I hope you can find her a good studio in Des Plaines."

"I wish *you* could be my teacher," I told her.

"Now wouldn't that be fun!" she laughed.

I could see from the corner of my eye that Miss Mendoza was looking at me. Maybe she was imagining me as her student. Before dinner, she had redone my hair. I wasn't her student, but when she had pulled my hair into a tight bun, I had imagined, just for those few minutes, that maybe I was.

After dinner I cleared the table and put the dishes into the sink to soak. Soon I would have to slip on rubber gloves and get to work. That was the only thing I hated about enchilada dinners—those messy plates that I had to scrub until my arms were limp. Then I remembered that our new house has a dishwasher, and

I did a jeté to celebrate. My days of scrubbing dishes by hand would soon be over!

But the dishwashing could wait tonight. Mom shooed me into the living room to be with all of them. I thought I would have to listen to Dad talk about his childhood and tell stories about working in the beet fields in Illinois. But I was wrong. He talked about picking apples in Washington, instead.

Mom rescued us when she asked Miss Mendoza, "Where's your father this evening?"

"Good question," Miss Mendoza responded. "He says he's playing dominos, but I think he must be up to something else."

Mom was wise at picking up signals. "You mean . . . a lady friend?"

Miss Mendoza nodded her head. "I think so," she said. Then she put her coffee cup down and got to her feet.

Wow, I thought. *Her dad's like sixty, or even older, and he has a girlfriend!*

Miss Mendoza complimented Mom's dinner and

said next time it would be *her* turn to cook for us. But now that Mom had reminded her, she needed to go out and see about her father.

"May I come?" I asked boldly. I was already on my feet.

Dad narrowed his twiggy eyebrows at me.

"Of course," Miss Mendoza said. "Is that all right with you? Elisa? Hector?"

"Can I, Mom? May I?" I tried to blink my eyes in a sorrowful way. "Pretty please?" I couldn't believe I was actually begging.

"Are you trying to get out of doing the dishes?" Mom asked.

I was insulted. "No, Mom, I'll do them when I come back. They're soaking right now."

Mom murmured, "OK, but take my phone, just in case." She went to her purse.

"Mom, we're only going three blocks," I protested.

"You never know when you might need it," she said, putting it in my pocket.

"I'll bring her back in half an hour," said Miss Mendoza. I grabbed my purple dance wrap as she shouldered her purse and led me to the front door.

Downstairs we ran into Victor sitting on the steps, examining his purplish fingers in the fading light.

"What's wrong?" I asked.

"It's gone," he labored to say. It seemed like he was ready to cry and I wondered if someone had stolen something from him.

"What's gone?" I asked.

"My raspada," he answered sadly. A Popsicle stick lay on the cement steps between his feet. Victor had pigged out on his Popsicle, and now he was sad that it was gone. He didn't deserve a second look!

Miss Mendoza and I walked up the street. Even though it was October, it was still warm, so lots of our neighbors were sitting on their steps. We said our hellos as we passed. I figured that some of them were wondering who Miss Mendoza was, and I knew that they would become gossipy when we were just out of earshot. That's how our neighborhood is!

"I know where my father is," Miss Mendoza said. A smile arched and deepened on her face.

We walked two blocks in silence. Her long strides had me almost running, and I could feel a pinch of pain in my side. I stopped once to tie my shoe and then had to run to catch up. At last we stopped and Miss Mendoza opened the door of the Senior Citizens Center—the same place where my dance class was scheduled to perform on Thursday. It was so bright inside that I had to cover my eyes.

"You're sure he's here?" I asked as we walked up the hallway.

She nodded her head. "Oh, yeah. He's here."

We cruised into the recreation room, where we found him playing dominos with a woman.

"Roberto Mendoza!" his daughter called.

I hadn't known that Mr. Mendoza's first name was Roberto, or that he could move so fast. He rose quickly to attention, and for a second I thought he was going to salute his daughter.

Both Miss Mendoza and I could see what was up. Mr. Mendoza was romancing his woman friend. She was dressed in a flowered shift. Her mouth was red with lipstick, her cheeks pinkish from a sweep of blush. She was no doubt trying her best to look good.

"I'll be right back," he muttered to the woman in Spanish. He seemed a little bit embarrassed at being caught and all, especially with me at Miss Mendoza's side. But I thought, *Hey, good for you, Mr. Mendoza!*

"Nice evening," Mr. Mendoza declared.

That was my cue to get lost. I went back out to the corridor to wait for them to finish their father-daughter talk. Miss Mendoza came out shortly.

Together we went down the steps and waited outside the Senior Citizens Center for Mr. Mendoza to join us.

"I knew the rascal was up to something," said Miss Mendoza. Then she told me she had sold her dance studio and moved from New York City to Chicago in order to take care of her father. He had fallen and hurt his hip, which was why he shuffled when he walked.

"*Ay, mi papi,*" Miss Mendoza sighed.

"Do you wish you were still in New York?" I asked.

She chewed the inside of her cheek. "No and yes. I like being with my father, but I do miss teaching."

So, come teach in Des Plaines, I nearly blurted out. But I checked myself. How could I ask her to do that?

"He doesn't really need any help," she said as she opened the door of the Senior Citizens Center for an elderly woman. "I can see that now."

That seemed like the truest thing I was going to hear all day. He didn't need *anyone's* help. When he exited the Senior Citizens Center a moment later, with his dominos under his arm, he was whistling a Mexican song. He gave his daughter a smile and patted my shoulder.

"Guess what!" he said.

Miss Mendoza hesitated for a moment before she asked, "Papi, what are you up to?" She propped her hands on her hips, the way my mom does when she means business.

"Come on—guess!"

"You lost at dominos?"

"No, something good. I'm going to have to buy a new suit."

We blinked at Mr. Mendoza, confused.

Smiling, he placed his hand over his heart and announced with a giggle, "I'm getting married."

4

A New Friend

I was surprised twice that evening. First, that Mr. Mendoza was getting married, and next because Mom and Dad had done the mountain of dishes for me! The next morning I was surprised again when, instead of going to church, we went to our new house with a load of stuff. It was the stuff that Mom thought too precious to load up in a truck—a painting she had bought in Mexico and the fancy dinner plates my parents had washed the night before. She also had her special loot—her jewelry and lots of boxes of shoes. Mom loves her shoes.

I brought along my most prized possessions—my folklórico skirts. And Dad? Dad took the baseball glove from his childhood.

"If I ever lost my favorite glove," Dad said as he maneuvered our van up one street and down another, "I would lose myself."

I understood what Dad meant. I could see that Mom did, too, even though Dad sounded like a poet who doesn't make sense.

We got lost in the new neighborhood.

"I think I take a left here," Dad argued with himself.

I was thinking, *No, it's right.* But I kept my mouth shut. I sat buckled in the back seat, turning over in my mind what Mr. Mendoza had said. Was he kidding about getting married? Miss Mendoza had seemed a little angry and had even stomped her foot when he announced the news in front of the Senior Citizens Center. But they hadn't discussed it any more, probably because I was there. Instead, we walked home in silence—except when Mr. Mendoza whistled.

In time, Dad found the house.

As he parked our van in the driveway, I had to admit that I liked our new house. It was prettier than our apartment building, and the neighborhood *was* quiet.

While Mom and Dad went happily inside, I stayed outside to size up the new place. I was still sorry about moving away from Chicago, but the house was growing on me. I felt happier than I had yesterday when I was here. I kicked through the fall leaves and tossed some into the air. I stopped when someone behind me chirped, "Hi."

I turned and there she was—the girl I had seen the day before from my bedroom window. Her brown hair was tied up in a ponytail. She wore another sweater that hid her hands, but she pulled up her sleeves when she caught me looking at them. Her fingernails were polished red, like she had dipped them in jam.

"Hi," I greeted her in return. I told her my name.

"Say that again," she said.

"MAR-EE-SOUL," I repeated, pronouncing each syllable slowly for her.

"Spell it?" she asked, confused.

I spelled it for her—Marisol, the name of my grandmother and, I think, the name of one of my Dad's girlfriends before he met Mom.

She said her name was Karen Johnson. I said there was a girl in my ballet folklórico troupe named Karen.

"You dance?" asked Karen. Happiness spread across her face as she stood on her tiptoes for a second.

"Yeah," I answered. "You, too?"

When she nodded her head, her ponytail bounced.

I realized I was starting to really like my new home. And I liked it even more when Karen invited me to her house—well, actually, to her front yard, where she had been raking leaves into three piles.

Each of the piles came up to my knees, but when we scooted and raked all of them together, the pile came up to our waists.

"What now?" I asked.

"This," Karen answered. She backed up, took six running steps, and jumped into the pile.

We raked the leaves into a pile again and then it was my turn. I took a running start and, holding my breath, flew into the pile. It was a total rush.

I got up, dizzy with happiness. Leaves crowned my hair.

"Cool!" I said.

We leaped into the pile a couple more times and then sat on the lawn, twirling leaves by their stems. "Look, they're dancing!" I said, laughing. "Just like us."

"Actually," Karen confided, "I'm not dancing anymore." She stopped twirling the leaf in her hand.

"Why not?" I asked.

"Our teacher got married and moved away."

This piece of news stopped me. Did that mean that there wasn't a dance studio here? I asked, "What kind of dance did she teach?"

"Everything," she answered. "You know, like tap, modern, jazz, ballet."

"I've tried some of those, but I'm not very good at ballet," I admitted.

"I'm sure you are," Karen said sweetly.

"Well, I keep trying, but if there's no ballet teacher, then I won't ever be able to get better," I said.

Then I told Karen about my ballet folklórico troupe, and that we were learning *El Caimán*. I jumped up, grabbed her hand, and pulled her to her feet. "Want me to teach you?" I asked.

Her smile lifted her cheeks and narrowed her eyes into shiny triangles as she nodded. She gazed over my shoulder at my house. "Do you have your dance stuff with you now? I love those costumes you wear. They're so pretty."

I told her that we hadn't moved in but that I had my folklórico skirts—the three that I owned—with me. Although we had known each other for only a few minutes, we were already friends. Without a word we took off running toward our houses—Karen flew up her steps and I flew up mine.

Minutes later, we reappeared with our dance stuff. First I showed her my Veracruz skirt, being careful not to let it drag on the lawn. Then we climbed up on her porch and I handed her my bright yellow Jalisco skirt. She'd brought out her favorite tutu and explained that her teacher had left it, along with some other costumes, for when—not *if*—another studio got started. The tutu was made of a deep purple tulle with purple and black lace.

"The last principal dancer who wore this was really beautiful," Karen told me. "I wanted to dance just like her, to *be* her." She paused. "I hope we find another teacher soon." I nodded, thinking that ballet would be fun if I could do it with Karen.

She pressed my Jalisco skirt up to her body and said, "Your skirts are so swirly!"

I held the tutu up to me. "This is soooo great," I gushed. I hadn't been doing ballet long enough to even dream of wearing a fancy tutu (I was still in a pink leotard!) but this was so gorgeous that I wished I *were* good enough to wear it. I tiptoed, like a ballerina. I arched my arms into a circle as if I were drawing the world. And there on the porch, holding on to that purple tutu, I started to get that excited feeling that I always get when I dance.

"I love this tutu . . . and this color!" I said.

"Me, too," Karen said. "Actually, I love everything about ballet. I don't even mind the hard work it takes because I know every ballerina has to go through that. That's what my teacher said. She was so terrific. I really miss her." Karen looked a little sad. "You would have liked her."

I nodded sympathetically.

"Come on inside," Karen said, brightening. "I don't want us to get any of these dirty."

We gathered up our costumes and went into Karen's house. I was careful to wipe my feet. The floors were wood—good for dancing. They were shiny enough for me to see my face. Only the stairs were carpeted.

We stomped up the carpeted stairway to Karen's room.

"Wow," I exclaimed as I marveled at the shelves of stuffed animals. "You sure have a lot of stuffed animals."

"That's because I have a lot of uncles who spoil me."

"I like your bed," I said. It had a canopy, and the bed-spread was frilly, like the lace on my Veracruz costume.

I walked to the window that faced my bedroom.
I could see Dad doing something in there. He seemed
really tall, much taller than usual. When he moved
again and was suddenly shorter, I realized that he had
been standing on a chair to change a lightbulb.

Then I saw him hold up his baseball glove and
start yapping it open and closed, like the mouth of
an alligator. I could imagine Mom laughing at him.
Crazy Dad, I thought.

Karen and I tried on each other's dance outfits.
When Karen twirled, my Jalisco skirt flared beautifully
and slowly collapsed like a parachute.

"You look great!" I said. "Like you were born for it!"

I twirled, but the stiff tutu didn't flutter. It was the
first time I'd ever put on a tutu, and I felt different—almost
like a real ballerina. I was busy imagining myself floating
across the stage as the Sugarplum Fairy in *The Nutcracker*
when Karen did a hitch kick. I came back to reality
and did one, too, and suddenly we were a chorus line—
Karen and I kicking our legs up and laughing. But our

laughter stopped when Karen's mom appeared in the doorway.

We're busted, I thought.

"What do we have here?" her mother asked, smiling. "The Rockettes?"

"I know a real Rockette!" I said. "Only now she lives in Chicago."

Karen's mom held up my Veracruz skirt and cooed, "It's very pretty." Then she brought from her apron pocket four homemade oatmeal cookies. We took off our dance things before sitting cross-legged on the bed with our cookies. I ate mine carefully, with my hand under my mouth to catch the crumbs. I wanted to show I had grown-up manners, though when Karen turned her back I vacuumed up the crumbs from my palm.

"Which do you like better?" Karen asked.

"What do you mean?" I said. For a moment, I thought she was asking about the cookies.

"You know—ballet, or ballet folklórico, or jazz?"

Instinctively, I shrugged. "I like them all, but ballet is definitely the hardest."

"I think it's hard for everyone," Karen replied, "but I just absolutely, positively love it. I was born to be a ballerina."

With a twinkle in her eye, she grabbed my hand, pulled me off the bed, and started spinning me like a top. I grabbed her other hand and then we were turning around together face-to-face. Next, without even planning it, we locked arms and did some crazy hoedown turns before we collapsed, giggling, on the floor.

On the drive home, I thought about Karen, the Rockettes, and Miss Mendoza. Since Karen's teacher was gone, maybe Miss Mendoza really *could* start a studio in Des Plaines! She could rent a studio with lots of mirrors. There would be lines of girls doing hitch kicks to the ceiling. And I would be one of them.

Mom asked about Karen and I told her what I knew: that Karen was a fourth grader like me, that she was also a dancer, that she had more stuffed toys than a small toy store, and that her mom was nice. I also said that Mrs. Johnson was a good cook.

"How do you know that?" Mom asked.

I held up two oatmeal cookies nearly as large as Frisbees and gave one to each of my parents. "She sent these home for you two," I said.

When we got home—back to our apartment— I found Victor on the front steps. He was sitting with his cheeks in his palms. A Popsicle stick lay at his feet. I noticed the wooden stick had a couple of teeth marks.

"It's all gone, huh?" I asked. His eyes appeared as if they might leak big, fat tears.

He nodded his head.

I ran inside to my bedroom, where I listened for the sound of dancing feet. I heard nothing but the quiet shuffling of Mr. Mendoza's slippers. Then I heard the squeak of a recliner—no doubt Mr. Mendoza had bailed into its soft spot.

"He's getting married," I told my stuffed animals. I pictured him walking down the aisle of St. Mary's Church in his ... slippers, those fuzzy things that resemble raccoons.

Then I heard Miss Mendoza's swift steps. She was home after all.

Excited, I hollered as I danced through the living room toward the front door, "Mom, I'll be right back." Mom was writing down messages from the answering machine.

I skipped up the flight of steps to Mr. Mendoza's apartment and knocked. I heard soft steps and in the next second felt the breeze of the opening door.

"Hi," Miss Mendoza greeted me. She was dressed in black dance pants and a tee shirt. She told me to come in, and I rushed in like the wind.

"I have an idea," I burst out as I stepped into the living room.

Miss Mendoza raised her eyebrows as if to ask,

"And what is that?"

I gazed over at Mr. Mendoza asleep in his recliner with a magazine in his lap. I was amazed. He had just sat down in his recliner three minutes ago and already he was asleep. His mouth was issuing a snore. His glasses had slipped down his nose.

"Let's go into the kitchen," I suggested, not wanting to wake him up. I remembered the kitchen very well. When I was six, Dad had made me help get Mr. Mendoza's kitten from under the stove—my arms were really skinny, and they could reach far.

Miss Mendoza led me into the kitchen, where we sat at the table.

"OK, what big ideas do you have, sweetheart?" Miss Mendoza asked.

She read my mind, I thought. *We're in tune! She knows I've got a big idea!*

"You know we're moving," I said.

She nodded her head.

"But it's not far away." My attention was drawn briefly

to the clock on the far wall. It was owl shaped—the eyes swiveled left, then right, with each second. "Well, I really don't want to move for a zillion reasons."

"Give me one," Miss Mendoza said.

Only one? I thought. I sat up straight. "For one, I won't be able to take dance anymore, ballet or ballet folklórico. My friend there—her name is Karen—said that the dance teacher in Des Plaines moved away. And I was thinking ..."

I let my words hang in the air before I continued.

"I was thinking that maybe ... since your father's getting married and all ... maybe you can start a dance studio out there, where we're moving." When Miss Mendoza didn't clap her hands together and scream, "What a great idea!" I added, "And I can be your first student." I told her again about Karen's teacher closing her studio, and how I had checked the telephone book at our new house and found no other dance studio listed near our house.

Miss Mendoza munched her lower lip, scraping

away some of her lipstick. "Now, how would I get there to teach? I don't drive. And it's far, Des Plaines."

I pointed out the window. "It's not *that* far," I said. "You can practically see it from here!"

"Great. You're not only good at dancing but brilliant at geography," she said, laughing.

I laughed, too. "It's really not far, and you *can* see it from here!" I answered. "Dad got lost only once."

Miss Mendoza smiled. She rose and went to the kitchen sink for a glass of water. She asked if I wanted something to drink, but I smacked my lips to assess my thirst. I shook my head. "No, thanks, I'm fine."

Miss Mendoza returned to the kitchen table.

Then I said, "You can move in with us. We have plenty of room. There's even an extra bedroom." I told her how big our house was, and that it had lots of trees, and I even described the piles of leaves and how Karen and I had jumped in them.

"Yes, I see." Miss Mendoza reached over and plucked a leaf that was caught in my hair. She twirled it between her fingers, making it dance. "Sweetie, you're such a dreamer." Her eyes cut to the doorway and the not-so-faraway sounds of snoring. "What about my dad?" she asked.

"But he's getting married," I repeated. "He doesn't need you now. You said so yourself. And I *really* need a dance teacher."

"I don't think he's really getting married, Marisol. He's a dreamer *and* a big flirt, and is always saying things like that." She said that she had to stay with him and that she would find a job nearby. "And even if he does get married, I'm probably going to stay here in Chicago. You'll find a teacher—and a good one, I'm sure."

I felt what Victor felt when his raspada was all gone—sad. What was I going to do now?

We sat in silence. The owl-shaped clock swiveled its eyes. I hung my head down and, for some reason, I began to swivel my eyes as well. The funny thing was that when I raised my face, I saw that Miss Mendoza's own eyes were keeping rhythm to the clock, too.

We laughed. We laughed hard and with our mouths open. And we laughed even harder when Mr. Mendoza shuffled into the room asking, "What's so funny?"

"The clock," we answered.

Mr. Mendoza slowly raised his face to the clock. He studied it for the longest time before mumbling, "Yeah, it is a pretty funny clock." He chugged in his slippers back to the living room, grumbling that we should have awakened him for his favorite program, *Animal Adventures*.

I had to try a second time. "Well, what do you think?" I asked Miss Mendoza. Of course I am a dreamer, but without dreams, what is life?

"About starting a dance studio? Out in the suburbs?" She looked out the window. "I can see you're a quick study, Marisol. And determined. It'd be fun to be your teacher, but I can't."

I thought I had lost her, but then she kept talking. She said she realized that her father wasn't as helpless as he had described in the letter that he had written her, the one that had brought her back home. "You know what he did before he sent that letter?" she roared. "He sprinkled some water on it and said it was his tears." She slapped her thighs. "Can you believe that? He's such a bad boy. *Muy malo.*"

We heard the sounds of an elephant trumpeting on the television.

"But what am I going to do if I don't have a dance studio? Karen says they don't teach dance at her school," I said quietly. "And Mom won't talk about it. How am I supposed to be a dancer if I have no one to teach me?"

"And who's this Karen again?" Miss Mendoza asked.

"Karen lives next door," I repeated. Again my arm swung up to point in the direction of Des Plaines. "Karen does modern and ballet and stuff."

"And *stuff*?"

I could see that I had insulted Miss Mendoza. "You know, traditional ballet and the kind of dancing *you* do." I propped a grin on my face. "Come on, can't you at least visit my new school to see if you can teach there, after school or something?"

"You mean, teach my 'stuff'?"

"I mean DANCE!"

"Well, you can't just do the 'stuff' you like. I might consider teaching you folklórico if you keep up your traditional ballet."

"But how? There's no school there!"

"You'll find one if you're serious."

We grew silent. We could make out the laughter of a hyena on the television and then the laughter of Mr. Mendoza.

Silence, more silence. The owl's eyes went left, right, left, right.

"So, do you want to try some of my 'stuff' right now?" Miss Mendoza asked.

Before I could answer, Miss Mendoza left the room and returned with a glittery pink top hat and a cane. She also produced a pair of shoes and said, "These were mine when I was your age. Go ahead and put 'em on."

I took the shoes, noticing the toes were a little scratched, and put them on. They were a perfect fit. I took a few steps across the floor and into the living room and felt like I was walking on spoons.

"I like the sound," I said, beaming my happiness down to the tap shoes. Then Miss Mendoza wrapped a pink fringed skirt around my waist, and we started to dance. Miss Mendoza took my hand. She told me to tap, tap, tap the toe, and then land on the heel. Shuffle right, shuffle left, then a big finish with the cane on the arm and top hat aloft.

We danced for nearly an hour. "I feel like a Rockette!" I said. We were all smiles. If I were a flower, I would have been blooming at that moment.

"OK, that was your first lesson," Miss Mendoza said with her eyes twinkling. "And I'm not even going to charge you."

I took off her tap shoes and the pink skirt and began to stretch on the floor—my head touched my knees.

"You have a nice stretch," Miss Mendoza remarked.

"Once I was able to put my leg behind my head," I said proudly.

"When was that?" Miss Mendoza asked suspiciously.

"When I was a baby. That's what Mom says."

Miss Mendoza laughed and asked, "And did you put your toes in your mouth?"

"Probably," I said and laughed with my hand over my mouth.

Then we sat in silence. Miss Mendoza asked, "What's your friend's name again, the one at your new place?"

"Karen."

With her head against the back of the sofa, Miss Mendoza looked up at the ceiling. "And where is Des Plaines?" she asked, still breathless from dancing.

I had her!

I pointed again, and we both laughed.

"But it's only *maybe,* Marisol," she insisted.

5

Two Square Champ

Monday morning I stepped off the school bus. I stuck out my tongue and tasted a raindrop that had fallen miles and miles from up above. The previous night the sky had turned as cold and gray as the cement I now skipped on in my pink sneakers. For the first time, I realized that I was going to lose a lot of my friends. I was going to lose the best teachers in the world and even Mr. Perez, the janitor, who had gotten my backpack off the roof the time a stupid boy threw it up there.

"Hi," Sara yelled from the schoolyard, where she was locking her bike. She was lucky that she lived only five blocks away and her parents let her ride her squeaky bike. Of course, her older brother, Enrique, led the way, splashing through puddles on rainy days.

"Hey," I greeted her in return.

We spent a few minutes examining each other's lunches—I had a turkey sandwich and potato chips that I would smash after I put them in the sandwich. Sara had the same thing, except her potato chips were barbecue-flavored. We would eat our lunches on a bench with a couple of sparrows waiting around for crumbs.

But at that moment food wasn't really in my thoughts. I had something serious to announce.

"We're moving," I told Sara in a whisper.

Sara didn't seem to understand. She was snacking on a carrot stick.

So I repeated myself.

"What do you mean?"

"I mean, like, we're moving away. My parents bought a house."

She stopped munching her carrot.

"Why?" she asked.

"Because my mom and dad think it's better."

But better than what? I argued to myself. *What's better than my friends, my neighborhood, and my bedroom?* I felt like a traitor. Sara and I meandered toward our classroom, arm in arm, best friends forever and ever. I slipped a Halloween candy (Mom had let me open a bag of candies) into Sara's pocket without her knowing.

The bell rang.

"Don't move away," Sara begged as she released my arm.

I didn't know what to say except, "I don't want to, but I have to."

That period we did math and had silent reading. When I looked across the classroom, Sara flashed the mini candy bar at me and smiled. But when she flashed it a second time, our teacher, Miss G, called out, "Sara! What do you have?"

"Nothing," Sara answered and guiltily bit her lip.

Miss G walked over and asked Sara to open her fist. The candy bar rolled onto her desk.

"So this is nothing?" asked Miss G.

"Well . . ." Sara fumbled for an explanation. "It's something now, but later, after I eat it, it'll be nothing."

Miss G didn't appreciate her explanation.

Then Sara squeaked, "Marisol's moving."

Miss G warned Sara not to eat candy in class and cast a look at me across the classroom. I was sitting with my back straight, pretending to be reading. I was a little nervous because that was my candy. Maybe I was in trouble as well.

"Marisol," Miss G called as she took a few steps toward my desk.

Was I busted? I raised my face from my book.

"Marisol, may I talk to you at recess?" She turned and handed the candy bar back to Sara and returned to her desk, where she hovered over our math quizzes.

At recess, the class ran for the door, screaming for freedom. I stayed behind.

"Your mother said you might be moving," Miss G said. She picked up the wooden apple on her desk. She got it last year when she was voted best teacher in the school. The apple looked real, down to the little green leaf on its stem.

"She did?" I responded. Do parents and teachers talk behind our backs? I envisioned them talking late at night on the telephone. Mom would have been on her cell phone, of course.

"About a month ago," Miss G explained. "You're moving to Des Plaines. You'll like it there."

"How do you know?" *Dang,* I thought. *Am I rude or what?*

"Because *I* live there," she answered. She didn't seem hurt by my questioning tone. She came out from behind her desk and sat in one of the student desks. She looked really big in that desk. "It's a nice place."

She lives there! I thought.

"I am sorry, though," Miss G continued, "that I'll be losing my star student."

For a moment I was baffled about who the star student could be. Then it dawned on me that she was referring to me! I would have blushed, but my cheeks were already pink from the heat. I had taken off not only my jacket but my sweater, too.

"I really don't want to move," I whined.

"I know it's hard, Marisol."

"I'm going to miss our school." Boy, it was really embarrassing, but I could feel my eyes brimming with tears. And was that a hiccup of sorrow rising in my throat? "I'm going to miss my friends and my neighborhood," I added. I pictured Victor sitting on the steps of our apartment building eating two Popsicles—one for each sticky hand!

Miss G got me a Kleenex, which I rubbed under my nose.

"And if we move, then I can't take dance anymore." I told her there were no studios in Des Plaines and probably no dance classes at my new school.

"But do you know that for sure?" Miss G asked. "Maybe they'll have classes there." She shifted in her seat. "Or you can study karate or something else."

"But dance is what I love. There's no ballet folklórico,

and not even any regular ballet there," I said. "I asked Miss Mendoza if she wanted to move with us and start her own studio. She said maybe, but I think she just said that to make me go away."

Miss G didn't respond immediately. I could hear the big clock on the wall *clack, clack* each long second. Then she asked, "Who is Miss Mendoza?"

"Mr. Mendoza's daughter. She lives with him, but he's getting married." I babbled about trying to get Miss Mendoza to move to Des Plaines to open a dance studio like the one she used to have in New York.

Miss G appeared confused.

"She used to live around here," I explained, "but she went to New York City to become a Rockette."

"Gloria Mendoza?" Miss G asked, rising like a big mountain from that tiny desk. Her face became red with excitement. "She used to be *my* dance teacher way back."

"Way back?" I asked.

"When I was your age," Miss G said. "She's back in Chicago?" She had a dreamy look on her face and then a look like she might cry.

Was I going to have to get Miss G a Kleenex and pat her on her back and say, "There, there, it's not so bad"? I was prepared for such a scene, but it turned out that Miss G was ready to shed tears not from sadness but from happiness. It also turned out that the classroom phone rang just then, and Miss G got up to answer it.

"We'll talk more later, Marisol," she said as she picked up the receiver.

I left the classroom and played tetherball for exactly thirty-two seconds, which was enough time to beat Victor. He was using only one hand because he was eating a candy bar. Then it was back to class!

I wondered why Miss G was so excited. Then it came to me. I mean, if I hadn't seen my teachers—either Mademoiselle Juliette or Maestra Davila—in years and years, I guess that I would be excited to discover that one of them was back in the neighborhood. Still, I didn't really think about it. I ate my lunch with Sara, spanked my hands free of potato chip crumbs, and got to work.

What kind of work was that? Two Square. I was the Two Square champion of our school. I hadn't lost a single game in six weeks. I played against everyone—rough boys, tall girls, everyone.

"I'm going to win today!" some boy shouted.

Yeah, right, I thought.

I beat him seven to one and the next boy seven to two, and then I beat three girls, who drifted away to the monkey bars. Before lunch recess ended, a girl I had never seen before stepped into the square. She had a ponytail like Karen's and glasses that were shiny bright. When she smiled, I could see her retainer.

"Ready, spaghetti?" I asked.

"Ready, Freddy," she answered. "Your serve."

She leaned her body over, ready for a swift serve. I palmed the rubber ball wickedly, and she returned it just as fast. We slapped the ball back and forth. Our hair bounced wildly as we engaged in battle for the first point.

The first point belonged to the new girl. The second point went to her, too.

She's tough, I grumbled to myself. Still, I served up some hot shots and got the score back to two to two. I realized I had met my match. This girl had a powerful serve and was quick on her feet. I noticed that the toes of her tennis shoes were worn. Wherever she was from, she must have been the champ there.

A crowd formed around us. I took the lead, five to three, but she came back with deadly corner shots that had me sweating. She regained the lead, six to five.

"Time out!" I yelled, breathing hard. I peeled off my sweater.

The new girl peeled off her sweater, too.

"Ready!" I yelled. I leaned low to the ground and a little to the right to make her believe that I was expecting a serve to the right corner. But I was really expecting a serve to the left—and there it came, as fast as any serve I had faced. I hit the ball with the heel of my palm, and my return almost went out. We battled for three minutes

before I got her with a slap shot on the toe of her left shoe.

My serve! We were tied six to six. I could feel the warm breathing of the kids huddled around us.

We were battling when the bell rang. The kids screamed as they ran for their classrooms, leaving the new girl and me behind, slowing our game to polite pats to each other's squares. I tucked the Two Square ball under my arm.

A tie game.

I was about to ask her her name when the principal's whistle screamed. We raced to our classes, I to fourth grade and she (I gulped as I realized she was younger than I) to the third-grade class. I was on my way out, and she was going to be school champ for a long time.

At home, I did my homework perched on my trunk at the bedroom window. It felt like the best place in the world and was, I guess, my own private world. I could see Victor playing basketball with some boys. I could see a neighbor working on his car. His shirtsleeves were rolled up and his Cubs baseball cap was turned backward. The morning's gray skies had finally cleared, and now it was warm again. It had turned into a perfect fall day in the neighborhood—*my* neighborhood. How could I leave this place?

Mom had taken Monday off to pack, but Dad had gone to work. I imagined him fixing one of the trains that carried commuters from one part of Chicago to another part—probably even to Des Plaines. Everything seemed to be in motion—trains, cars, people on the sidewalk, the jets overhead, and even my sneaky cat, Rascal. He had been basking in the last rays of sunlight on the neighbor's brick wall. But just as I looked up from a math problem, that four-legged troublemaker was slinking slowly toward a bird.

I threw open the window and yelled, "Rascal!"

Everyone gazed up at me. Victor and his basketball friends, the neighbor with his car tools, a man passing on his bicycle, and the mail carrier with her sack of letters—they all craned their necks.

"I mean my cat!" I yelled to the crowd. "RASCAL, get away from that bird!"

The bird darted over a fence. From there it settled on the telephone line. And from there I don't know, because down in the street I saw my teacher and Miss Mendoza walking arm in arm, just like Sara and I do.

How did my teacher know where Miss Mendoza lives? I wondered. Then I figured that teachers know a lot of stuff, like where we live and when our birthdays are and stuff like that. That's why the teachers' lounge is off-limits to kids. The teachers disappear into the lounge. There they drink coffee, gobble doughnuts, and talk about us during recess—or so I imagine.

But this was amazing! Miss G had located her former teacher within a few hours after school.

"Hey!" I yelled to them.

When they stopped and looked up, I ducked my head. It was rude to call "hey" and then duck out of sight! I was caught like a rat when I heard Miss Mendoza yell, "Marisol!"

"YES!" I yelled without showing my face. I started to giggle. I felt like I was playing hide-and-seek.

"Come down here, *por favor!*"

Was I in trouble? Impossible! After all, I had been doing my homework and not goofing around in the street, like Victor. Maybe they were mad because of Rascal, my bird-stalking cat. Yes, that must be it.

But when I hurried down and met them on our apartment building's stoop, I was greeted with a hug from Miss Mendoza, who said, "I didn't know Clara was your teacher."

I blinked at Miss Mendoza.

"Who's Clara?"

They laughed with their hands in front of their mouths.

"Your teacher, mi'ja."

I didn't know Miss G's first name. Teachers' first names are a secret, like the combination to the lock on Sara's bicycle. (OK, I know the combination to that lock, but nobody else does.)

"So, this is where you live?" Miss G inquired.

"Right here," I answered. "And that's my bedroom." Even though it was only four thirty in the afternoon and still light out, I could see some of the stars glowing on the ceiling. Then my cat pranced up and nudged his head against my knee. "This is my cat." Then Victor came up to see what was going on. "And this is Victor." Then my neighbor Mrs. Maroni opened her front door and slapped a rug on the railing of the porch. Dust flew into the air. "That's Mrs. Maroni—she has the cleanest house around."

I stopped my inventory when I caught sight of Mr. Mendoza walking arm in arm with the woman from the Senior Citizens Center. I suspected that Miss Mendoza might huff and puff about her dad. I gulped and broke away from them. "Well, back to my homework."

I raced back into our apartment and hurried to my bedroom window. From that vantage point I could see all four of them—Miss G, Miss Mendoza, Mr. Mendoza, and his girlfriend—huddled together like umpires in a baseball game.

Were they talking about me? Miss G looked up at my bedroom, and then Mr. Mendoza raised his hand. They were up to something and were sneakier than my cat, who, I noticed, was creeping toward a pigeon in the gutter.

"RASCAL!" I yelled.

Rascal ran away and the four broke apart like umpires. They had made a call. If it involved me, was I safe or out?

6

Surprise!

Tuesday is corn-dog day. Wednesday is pizza and salad day, and every Wednesday the server winks at me as she scoops extra black olives onto my salad. She knows I love olives, especially green ones—though black ones are good, too. Today I sat down next to Sara and fitted the olives on the ends of my fingers. I started to eat each one slowly. But I stopped suddenly and leaped out of my chair.

"*Dang!*" I yelled. I jumped up, and the olives sprang from my fingers and rolled under the cafeteria table.

The principal, Mrs. Harris, looked up and lowered her reading glasses to the end of her nose, scanning the cafeteria for the loudmouth. She took three steps in my direction, her hand ready to curl a "come here" finger to me. But just then her walkie-talkie squawked, and she left the cafeteria. I was safe.

"What's wrong?" Sara asked.

"My skirts! They're at the new house!"

We had ballet folklórico practice right after school for tomorrow's performance at the Senior Citizens Center. Without a skirt, how could I dance? How could I twirl without feeling foolish? It would be like going to school in pajamas—way embarrassing!

Sara tossed an olive into her mouth, chewed, and slurred, "What are you going to do?" She hadn't swallowed what she was chewing.

"Do? I'm going to . . ." But smarty-pants me didn't have an answer.

"You've got a phone, right? Call your mom. Maybe she can drive to the new house and get your skirts."

"Yeah, maybe," I mumbled. But would she? Mom and Dad were cleaning the apartment and packing clothes and books. They were taking down pictures from the walls and sorting through all the things in our apartment. The movers were going to come on Saturday. If I called to ask, it would be pestering my parents when I knew they were really busy.

After leaving the cafeteria I didn't bother to play Two Square—everyone said the new girl was already taking over as the champ. That was OK with me. Instead, I hung out with Sara at the wooden play structure in the far corner of the schoolyard.

"I shouldn't have taken my skirts to the new house!" I cried.

"I'll lend you one of mine. Mom's making me new skirts, so I've got enough to share."

Sara is the best friend ever!

Still, I was mad at myself for forgetting my skirts. I climbed the wooden play structure and had a view of the school I loved so much. I could feel myself already missing it.

I mentioned to Sara that I had seen Miss G on my street.

"No way!" Sara crowed.

Seeing Miss G outside my house had been like seeing a teacher in the supermarket buying tomatoes or toothpaste—unreal. Teachers don't go out and buy things. It seems as if they live in the classroom or just wait at home for the beginning of a new school day.

"What was she doing there?" Sara asked.

"I don't know, but she was with Miss Mendoza."

Sara seemed to think deeply before she inquired, "Who's Miss Mendoza?"

"She's my neighbor, silly. Mr. Mendoza's daughter—the dancer. I told you about her." Then I told Sara about how Miss Mendoza had helped teach Miss G's dance classes.

"Like Maestra Davila is our teacher, huh?" Sara said.

"Exactly, my young friend!" I answered with a British accent. "I say, you are so astute."

"What's 'astute'?" Sara asked.

I stopped my British accent and answered, "It's . . . it's . . ." I didn't know. It was a word I had picked up watching a movie about two English sailors on a deserted island. "It's about seeing far away."

"Far away," Sarah repeated dreamily.

"Yes, far away, I think."

Sara gazed into the distance with her eyes bugged out. "Yeah, maybe I am astute," she said, pointing. "Here comes the principal."

I turned and spotted Mrs. Harris headed in our direction.

"I wonder who she's looking for," Sara asked.

"YOU!" said Mrs. Harris.

Sara and I looked around us from the height of the wooden play structure. There was nobody else within thirty feet.

"YOU!" Mrs. Harris cried a second time.

Again we swiveled our heads from left to right.

"Who's she talking to?" I asked.

"I don't know," Sara said. "I'm astute, like you said, but I can't see everything."

The YOU turned out to be me. Mrs. Harris was

mad because I had left the olives under the cafeteria table and the first graders had smeared them into an oily paste on the floor. She made me go back to the cafeteria to wipe up the mess they had made.

"There," I groaned, tossing the mess of paper towels into the garbage can. But lucky me, I had found a quarter. I pocketed it after a couple of private games of heads or tails.

But that was not the last I saw of Mrs. Harris.

Just as I was ready to sit down in class and work on my math, I heard a voice over the loudspeaker squawk, "Marisol Luna, please report to the principal's office."

Now, wait a minute! I grumbled to myself. *What could Mrs. Harris want now?* Did she want the quarter I had found? Maybe we could flip for it.

Sara looked over at me and shrugged her shoulders.

Outside the office, I had to wait on a bench with Victor. He had gotten in trouble for eating candy in class.

"What are you here for?" Victor asked. He had chocolate at the corners of his mouth. This would be evidence enough for him to have to pick up litter after school, which was the punishment for eating in class.

"I don't know." And that was the truth.

Victor asked if it was true that I was moving away.

"Yeah," I answered. I was picking at a sliver in my palm I had gotten from the wooden play structure.

"Can I have your cat?" Victor asked.

Have my cat! I thought. *Is he crazy?*

"No, Rascal is going with us," I replied.

"Can I have your dog, then?" Victor asked.

What dog?

"No, you can't have my dog because I don't have one."

Victor appeared baffled. "You don't have a dog?" he asked. He had the look of a kid who had just dropped his ice cream cone.

I told him no, that I didn't have a dog, hamster, parrot, rat, or even a rubber duck for my bath. "I just own one splendid cat," I bragged.

"I'm always hearing barking sounds from your apartment."

Barking sounds? I wondered. Then it dawned on me. It must have been Dad he had heard barking. Dad has recently gotten into rap, and his favorite song is one with bow-wow sounds. I would have explained this to Victor, except that he was called into the vice-principal's office and I was called into the principal's office.

"Hi, Mrs. Harris," I said, greeting her brightly.

Mrs. Harris peered over her reading glasses.

"Miss Luna, please come in. Sit down."

I climbed into a large chair in front of her desk. My legs barely hung over the edge.

"Boy, this chair is really big." When I leaned back, it squeaked. "I think it needs oiling." I wondered whether squished olives could be used as a sort of oil.

"Never mind about the chair, Miss Luna."

Good, I thought. *That's one less thing I have to worry about.*

Mrs. Harris worked her fingers into a steeple as she

leaned toward me. Sort of scared, I thought of pushing myself away from her desk and running out of her office. "How long have you been at our school?" she asked.

"Since I was little," I answered.

"What do you mean, 'Since I was little'? You're still little."

"Oh," I replied. "Then since I was really little."

Mrs. Harris straightened up, released her fingers from her steeple, and laughed.

I laughed, too, but just a little. I wanted to show her that I agreed with whatever was funny, even if I didn't know what it was.

"Are we going to lose one of our best students?" she asked.

For a second I wondered who that student was. Then I realized she was talking about me.

Mrs. Harris tapped a pencil against a pile of papers. The tap was nearly in time with the big-faced clock on the wall. And me? I swung my legs as I waited for

Mrs. Harris to finish whatever she wanted to say. She seemed to be stalling.

"We'll miss you," she said finally. "But we're going to remember you."

Remember me? I thought of the time that I, along with a stupid boy in my class, put gum in my hair for fun. Would she remember that? Or the time I ate four ice cream sandwiches during lunch and got sick?

As I walked back to my classroom, I could hear Mexican music. The song was "La Bamba." My toes wiggled to the rhythm of the music and my legs skipped.

"Calm down," I commanded my body parts. But my upper body began to sway. It couldn't help itself, especially since the music got louder as I approached the classroom. When I entered the room, the music suddenly stopped. The students yelled with their mouths open, like birds, "Surprise!"

My hand leaped bird-like to my heart. My class was giving me a going-away party. My name was written in thirteen colors on the white board. Balloons tapped the ceiling as they moved in the breeze created by the floor heater.

So, I figured out, *Mrs. Harris called me into her office just so they could get ready for a celebration.*

Then there was a second surprise, this one coming from Miss G and Miss Mendoza, who popped up from behind the teacher's desk. Their cheeks were pink with makeup and their hair was pulled back into ponytails.

"You're dressed up," I squealed. Then it hit me. The dance steps I had heard the night before above my bedroom belonged to them. They must have been practicing. Every time I had gone to knock on Mr. Mendoza's door, the dancing had stopped. Now they were dressed in gorgeous ballet folklórico skirts. When they twirled, their skirts flared. Their bracelets chimed and the heels of their shoes clacked against our floor.

"*Ole!*" someone yelled.

We all laughed.

My classmates moved out of the way as Miss G and Miss Mendoza swished to the center of the classroom.

All the desks were pushed against the wall, and a cake spiked with candles sat on Miss G's desk.

Miss G and Miss Mendoza started dancing without music, their bodies swaying from left to right.

"OK, Sara," Miss G called out.

Sara pushed a button on the class boom box.

The two dancers faced each other and began to dance. After a few steps I recognized the dance as *El Saus y la Palma*. It is a simple dance, but one where you can observe all the small movements—the dip, the arm positions, the steps.

When the dance ended, we all clapped until our palms hurt. I'm sure all of us were thinking, *That's Miss G? The girl can really go!* We were surprised that our teacher could dance. It hadn't occurred to any of us that any teacher could dance!

"I can tell you're all surprised," Miss G said breathlessly. "You think I just correct papers."

"No, we don't," someone screamed. "You dance gooder than we thought!"

We all winced at the bad grammar of "gooder." Still, we understood that whoever had said it meant it as a compliment.

Miss G dashed from the center of the room. "Did you recognize the dance?" she asked me as she squeezed me in a hug.

"That was awesome!" I told Miss G, nodding. "You can join our troupe—*really!*"

"I'm a little rusty," she said as she caught her breath. Her cheeks were pink from the happiness rising inside her. She pulled a Kleenex from her sleeve and wiped her brow.

"Don't believe her," Miss Mendoza argued. "She was the very best dancer in the troupe way back when."

"Girl, you're just saying that," Miss G countered with a little head swagger.

"No, I mean it."

Miss Mendoza smiled. She turned to the other twenty-three kids in the class and clapped her hands. "We're going to do a little folk dance. Find a partner."

I expected the boys to moan, "No, it's for girls," so I was surprised when Robert, a boy who sat at the back of the class and was as shy as a pony, grabbed my hand. My instinct was to pull it away, but I didn't want to be rude.

We did a simple heel, toe, swing-your-partner kind of dance that Miss Mendoza called a Texas Spinner. It was like the square dances we sometimes did in gym class.

"You dance very well," I complimented Robert. And I meant it.

"Thank you," Robert replied. "Are you going to miss us, Marisol?"

A lump sprang up in my throat. *Miss you? Yeah, I'll miss everyone!* I thought. But I didn't have time to dwell on this sad thought. When I looked toward the classroom door, a man dressed in old clothes, a mask, and slippers stood there. It clearly was Mr. Mendoza.

"*Buenas tardes!*" he called out with a wave of his hand. He held onto a cane with the other hand.

"Buenas tardes!" we chanted in return.

There was also another man, this one dressed in a white Mexican costume. He too wore a mask. He tapped a cane as he entered the classroom.

"We're lucky to have some very special guests," Miss G said after she clapped her hands for our attention. "This is Miss Mendoza's father and a special friend here to do a dance for us."

Right away, I knew the dance: *Los Viejitos,* the dance of the old men. It's really funny and old-fashioned. It starts with the old men tapping their canes, pretending they can barely walk because of their age. They are supposed to be as old as the hills—no, as old as the stars and moon. No, even older. Older than the sandwich I once left under my bed until it had turned hard as a rock.

"If we fall, don't worry about us, *mis amiguitos,* my little friends," Mr. Mendoza wheezed. Stooped over, he shivered and coughed to make himself appear sickly. His legs seemed to tremble.

"Yes, don't mind us," the other dancer agreed.

To me, Mr. Mendoza's friend didn't seem old, and he certainly didn't seem sick. He faked a couple of coughs like I do when I have to clean up my bedroom. He sneezed a loud phony sneeze.

Miss Mendoza pushed the "play" button on our class boom box. The two dancers began to totter about the classroom, holding on to the desks and walls. They tapped their canes. They scratched their heads as if they had forgotten something important. They fell onto the floor and got up slowly. They shook and dusted themselves off. They played sword fighting with their canes and ended up stabbing themselves in the foot.

We laughed.

But I didn't laugh when Mr. Mendoza's partner stumbled toward me and almost stepped on my shoe!

The dancer staggered away and fell onto the floor again. The kids all shrieked with laughter. But he leaped to his feet when the music began to quicken. His steps were lively, as were Mr. Mendoza's. The two old men danced expertly.

"Come here, you beautiful *señorita*," Mr. Mendoza called to Miss G.

Miss G squealed.

The men danced together, stopping only when the song came to an end.

We all clapped, but my claps were really for Mr. Mendoza, not the other dancer. I mean, how dare that guy almost squish my toes! After all, my dancing feet are my future!

"Let's give them another round of applause," Miss G said enthusiastically.

The dancers muttered, *"Mil gracias*—a thousand thanks."

Mr. Mendoza pulled off his mask and wiped his brow.

"Take your mask off, too," someone screamed to the other dancer.

The dancer shook his head no.

"COME ON!" we all bellowed.

The dancer shook his head a second time and started

for the door. But some of the boys hauled him to the center of the classroom. They wanted this masked dancer to reveal himself. He threw his arms up.

"OK, OK," he sobbed. "You got me."

When he pulled the mask off his face, I couldn't believe it—it was Dad! He was sneakier than Rascal!

What are dads for except to love you and sometimes embarrass you? He did both that afternoon, and he did another really nice thing by staying with me after school. He watched me practice and even surprised me with something from the van—my skirts. He had figured out that I had left all of my skirts at our new house and knew that I would need one for the Senior Citizens Center performance.

The next day, Thursday, I sadly packed some of my toys and clothes before school. Dad stayed home to continue packing and to be there for the men who were coming later to haul away the furniture that we were donating to the Salvation Army. Then, after school, Dad picked me up and drove me to the Senior Citizens Center for our performance. Mom was going to meet us there.

Mr. Mendoza was sitting on a folding chair in the recreation room. His dominos were set up, but there was no one to play against him. He nodded and smiled when he saw me.

"Where's your—" I started to ask.

"*Mi novia?*" he completed for me. "My girlfriend?" He chuckled. "She's off shopping for a wedding gown. Why not?"

"You're really getting married?" I asked.

He nodded his large head. "Don't be jealous, mi'ja," he remarked playfully. "You're always going to be my number-one girl."

For a split second I pictured myself as a flower girl, tap dancing down the aisle.

Mr. Mendoza then said, "You look really pretty in your skirt."

"Gracias," I said. And I did feel pretty.

I twirled once and saw myself in the wall of mirrors on one side of the room. I turned back to Mr. Mendoza and said, "And you're a really good dancer. I can see where Miss Mendoza gets her talent."

From across the room, Maestra Davila clapped her hands. "*Danzantes!* Dancers! Let's line up."

I lined up for the last time with the Harrison Park Ballet Folklórico Troupe.

I waved at Mr. Mendoza and at myself in the mirrors. I wasn't sure if the wave meant "hello" or "goodbye." Maybe I should have been sad, but when the music came on with a blare, my body took over. My feet were happy, and my shoulders, my legs, and even my ponytail seemed to dance to their own sweet rhythms.

7

Saying Good-bye

I stayed home on Friday to help my parents, and because I didn't want to say good-bye all over again to my friends at school.

We packed more boxes, and then I went shopping with Mom. She was looking for two chairs to match the couch she'd already picked out. I liked being with Mom. I liked driving around during the day. I spotted a herd of boys who were walking home from school with what seemed like weights in their shoes. Their steps were really slow, as if their backpacks weighted them down.

And me? My own feet were jumpy. I was happy. I stuck my head out the van's window and let the wind whip my hair. I opened my mouth like a hippo and swallowed gobs and gobs of air, but I clamped my mouth shut when Mom warned, "You're going to swallow a fly if you keep that up."

Then it was Saturday—moving day. But first I had my final ballet class. I shooed Rascal from where he was sleeping in my dance bag, grabbed it and a bottle of water, and raced down to the van. Mom was dropping me at class early so that she could pick up the new chairs and have them at home when the movers came later in the day.

"Hello, Marisol!" Mademoiselle Juliette greeted me when I arrived before the rest of the class. She was at the *barre,* where she had a leg up and her head lowered to her knee. Her stretch was incredible. Mine was pretty good, and I knew that Miss Mendoza's was really good. But Mademoiselle Juliette's? Picture-perfect. After all, she had studied at an academy in Paris, and for three summers she'd been an assistant ballet mistress at the Royal Ballet School in London.

"*Bonjour,* Mademoiselle," I answered in return and set

my bag on a bench. I took off my shoes and put on my dance slippers.

"So, you are moving after all?" Mademoiselle asked.

I nodded and reminded her that this was my last class with her. I said all this with a lump in my throat. I swallowed three times and the lump went down. If I had had wings on my shoulders, they would have slumped. That's how sad I felt.

Mademoiselle did quick sets of *relevés* and *echappés*. She rested for a moment and then fixed a look at me. "Your hair," she said directly.

Mademoiselle is picky about our hair being out of place. She says that messy hair means messy poise—and for her poise is just about everything. I redid my hair with a ribbon as she turned back to the barre. Up went her leg for another stretch.

"I hope you're going to keep practicing," she said to me in the mirror's reflection.

"Claro qué sí," I answered. I started to stretch, too.

"Claro qué sí," Mademoiselle echoed in her French

accent. She is learning Spanish from her boyfriend. She stopped and turned to face me.

"Marisol," Mademoiselle said, "you have a lot of talent." She reminded me of how, when I first came to her studio, my *battement frappé* was forced. "But now it is natural."

I liked the compliment, but I knew that my battement frappé isn't *really* natural. I am trying, but ballet is still a stretch for me.

"I hope I can find another ballet studio," I said. I told her about Des Plaines, and about Karen and how she likes to dance, too. But I also told her that Karen's teacher had moved away.

My feet then moved into *chaînes,* and Mademoiselle eyed the flashy work of my feet.

"*Très bien,*" she remarked and added something else in French I didn't understand. Finally, she translated: "Breathe. Do not hold your breath." Mademoiselle is also a stickler about breathing.

In truth, I *wasn't* sure whether I would be able

to continue with ballet or any kind of dancing in Des Plaines. Mom hadn't mentioned it, and even if she had, finding a studio didn't look promising. It was funny, because I was starting to really *like* ballet. I like a lot of things. Besides dance, there's soccer, volleyball, Two Square, and tetherball. Actually any competitive sport, except grungy football, gets me running. Heck, I would challenge Mr. Mendoza to dominos if I could get into the Senior Citizens Center.

So what should I do? I asked myself. *Everything!* answered the person who lives inside me.

Suddenly the ballet studio filled with other girls—including some tiny ones who came up to my waist. They ran to the barre and began doing series of *ronds de jambe,* one of the basic forms.

Meanwhile I continued stretching and practiced positioning my feet. When Mademoiselle clapped her hands and called out, "Positions," I ran to the barre myself. She scanned her students, asked for quiet, and announced, "Let's start with a few minutes of *développé.*" For us, this is a five-step movement that slowly stretches a leg outward.

I stood in preparatory position at the barre. I inhaled and exhaled. I glanced down at my ballet slippers. I saw that they were a little frayed and the toes were dark and scuffed from hours of practice.

"Lift," Mademoiselle called.

I couldn't help imagining that we dancers were a centipede as all of our legs lifted together into the air. We repeated the développé ten times and then switched to the right leg. This was followed by pliés and relevés.

"Backs straight," Mademoiselle called. "And breathe, please breathe, my buttercups."

The really little kids exhaled and inhaled, exhaled and inhaled. I laughed at the way they exaggerated everything, even the floor exercises that we did next.

Finally Mademoiselle clapped and called out, "Très bien, *mes petites*. That's all for today." Then she continued, "Now, as you know, next month we'll start preparing for *The Nutcracker*. We'll talk more about that next time."

Everyone started talking excitedly. My heart sank at the thought of missing the chance to perform. I'd started ballet after Mom and I saw *The Nutcracker* last year, and I had been hoping for a small part this year. I was still just a beginner, but even beginners got roles. Maybe now I'd never get to dance onstage, not even as a mouse or an angel, much less as a snowflake!

I stuffed my things in my bag at the end of class, my eyes filling with tears. As I said good-bye to some of the other girls in the class, Mademoiselle came over and gave me a small box.

"Open it when you get home," she said.

"*Merci*, Mademoiselle." I must have said it right, because she just nodded and gave me a hug. I hugged her hard and then ran to the car, wondering if I'd ever get the chance to be a real ballerina.

Sara came over Saturday, after her ballet class. "Where is everything?" Her words echoed off the walls of my empty bedroom.

But she knew. Most of my stuff—my stereo, the trunk with my special things, my precious posters, even my bed—was either taken apart or packed up for the move to the new place. I had only some boxes, a flashlight, a book, and my sleeping bag. With the stars on the ceiling, it was like camping.

"Packed," I answered.

Sara sat on the floor with her legs shot out in a V. She did a stretch and touched her head to her knee. Then she spied my bare foot and asked, "Where did you get that?"

"From Mademoiselle," I answered. She had given me a tiny toe ring to remind me of her and of my year at her studio.

"That was really nice of her," Sara murmured. Then she said, "Guess what!"

"Your dad got you a motorized scooter?" I had my feet pressed together and my hands were pushing my knees to the floor.

Sara laughed. "I wish!" She shook her head. "Nope. Mademoiselle told me this afternoon that she wants me to be one of the rats in *The Nutcracker*." Sara has been taking ballet longer than I have and is in a more advanced class.

"You go, girl!" I said as I cradled my leg and rocked it like a baby. "You'll be a perfect rat!" I released my leg and dropped my shoulders. "I just wish I could stick around for *The Nutcracker*. I asked Mom, but she said it'd be too hard to drive back and forth every weekend."

"You'll find another studio in Des Plaines," Sara said. She chewed at a fingernail.

"You think so?" I asked.

"I know so," she said. "I can just feel it. You're a dancer, and you need to dance. So you will," she declared simply.

Listening to her made me laugh, but then I got sad all over again that I had to leave Sara, my best friend, my main supporter, and my favorite dance partner.

Suddenly Dad called out, "Ballerinas!" He stood in the doorway with something closed up in his fist.

"Guess," he said, with a grin.

"Money," Sara answered.

He laughed as he unrolled his fingers. Sitting in his palm were a rubber ball and jacks.

"Where did you find them?"

"The same place I found some coupons, doctor bills, an old calendar, some broken crackers, a hairbrush, Rascal's collar, and other stuff."

"Behind the refrigerator?" Sara guessed.

"You got it."

How many times had Dad rolled the refrigerator away from the wall to let me search for something? One time I was looking for a plastic ring I'd lost. After Dad grunted and jiggled the refrigerator from its place, I found a real ring. I mean, one with a stone!

Dad challenged us to jacks, and we played on the living-room floor. I was surprised by Dad's stretch—he can almost touch his head to his knee!

And not only is Dad limber, but he can really play jacks. He beat me and then beat Sara, and he would have beat Mom, except she refused the challenge. She was going over her list of boxes once more before the moving truck came.

"Let's play again," I challenged. He had already beaten me five times, but I felt lucky this time.

"You're sure?" he asked. He squeezed the rubber ball in his fist. A muscle in his forearm shimmered.

"I'm sure," I said.

"OK, once more before I take Sara home," he agreed. "The movers will be here soon."

I threw the jacks, and they spun like stars on the wooden floor. I took the rubber ball from Dad, squeezed it, and bounced it twice. Then it slipped away from my grip and seemed to hurry away. Rascal, who had been sleeping near Mom, woke with a start, narrowed his blue eyes at the ball, and pranced after it. He pushed it with his paw like it was a hockey puck. He rose up onto his back legs and gripped it in his mouth. He spat it out and whacked it again. Then he—how clever my cat is!—he hiked it like a football between his back legs.

The ball bounced off the radiator and ricocheted off the kitchen cabinets.

"Stop it!" I yelled, as Sara and I scrambled to our feet.

Rascal leaped after the ball and kicked it under— you guessed it—the refrigerator. Dad moaned, "Let's just let it stay there for the next family."

So we left the rubber ball there. And as for Rascal? He beat it outside when Dad opened the front door. Dad and Sara descended the steps for the five-block ride to Sara's home, but first Sara and I hugged each other and made our private promise that we would be friends for life.

8

D for Dance, R for Rascal

Rascal disappeared completely when the movers arrived. No matter how often I called out "Kitty, kitty, kitty, silly kitty," he didn't appear. I searched up and down the street, but Rascal was nowhere to be found.

Victor helped me search for him. Even Mr. Mendoza joined our search. Miss Mendoza helped, too, but only for a little while because she said she had an important appointment she couldn't miss.

"You be good," Miss Mendoza said after she gave me a squeezing hug and handed me an envelope. "I'll be seeing you in Des Plaines."

"You will?" I asked.

"Claro qué sí," she answered. "Remember that Clara

lives there, too." I reminded myself that Clara was Miss G, whom I was also going to miss big time.

"Only visiting?" I asked. "What about the dance studio?"

Miss Mendoza just smiled and said, "We'll see what happens . . . Now don't open that envelope until you're at home in Des Plaines."

I promised and blew her a kiss.

After Miss Mendoza hurried away, we continued our search-and-rescue mission for Rascal.

"Rascal!" I screamed. "Rascal! RASCAL!"

"*Travieso!*" hollered Mr. Mendoza through his cupped hands.

Travieso is Spanish for "troublemaker." I guess that's close to the meaning of "rascal." Still, my cat didn't respond to either Spanish or English. He didn't respond to Victor's promise of food: "I'll get you a hamburger with two patties." After half an hour, he upped it to two hamburgers. Victor is a true friend.

We hunted for my cat until finally Dad came

hunting for me. "Mi'ja, we have to go. Mom went with the movers. We'll have to come back to look for Rascal." It was starting to get dark. The streetlights had come on, and the truck with our furniture and things was long gone.

"See you," Victor said softly.

"See you, Victor."

Victor reached into his pocket and brought out a candy bar. He pressed it into my palm.

"Thanks, Victor," I said. He was sweeter than the candy.

"*Adios,* mi'ja," Mr. Mendoza said. His eyes seemed wet. "I'll watch for your cat."

I climbed into our van crying. I didn't look up as we pulled out of the neighborhood with our friends waving good-bye. My life on that street was over. My cat was gone. Who would ever know that those handprints on our sidewalk belonged to me, Marisol Luna, the one and only daughter of Hector and Elisa Luna?

I sobbed all the way to our new house. Dad repeated that we'd go back to look for Rascal, but then he was quiet for the rest of the trip and just let me cry as much as I needed to.

Karen came over to greet me with a hug and some of her mom's oatmeal cookies. I wiped my tears as we sat down for a few minutes in the darkness of our front yard. The grass was dewy and damp, and it smelled good.

"I couldn't find my cat, Rascal," I told her, hiccupping with another sob.

"You'll find him," Karen said. "Cats do that when they know they're going to move."

Even though Mom and Dad had promised to go back and look for him, I was heartbroken. I pictured poor Rascal shivering in the night.

I raked my eyes clean of tears and gradually stopped whimpering. We sat on the lawn in silence for a while, munching on our cookies, before I asked, "What's your school—*our* school—like?" I hugged my knees because it was getting cold. When I blew out my breath, a cloud hung in the air.

"Big," she answered. "But nice big."

"Are the teachers nice?" I asked.

"Really nice," she answered. "You'll like Mrs. Buckley. She's my teacher and she'll be yours, too. I found out that we're in the same class."

We sighed about not having a dance studio or even dance classes at school. I told her that I was trying to talk Miss Mendoza into opening a studio here.

"That would be cool," Karen said.

"Yeah," I said. "She knows all kinds of dance styles. And she wants me to be more serious about ballet."

We agreed that there was probably something *else* we could do, like volleyball or soccer, if Miss Mendoza decided not to open a studio. Maybe we could even join 4-H together.

"Better come in," Mom called from the front door. "You can see Karen tomorrow."

"Well, not tomorrow, but Monday. We're going to see my grandparents tomorrow," Karen said. But she didn't leave right away. Instead, we started talking about ballet and how maybe, with a new teacher and enough hard work, the two of us could make it onto the stage one day.

"We'll be stars," Karen said, and then she pointed up at the night sky. "Hey, I just saw a shooting star!"

We both lifted our faces toward the dark sky then and waited for another star to shoot past. One did! Then we screamed when yet another one followed seconds later. I'd never seen *any* shooting star before, and now I'd just seen two of them! I decided that this is a true benefit of not living near quite so many city lights.

Mom came to the door and called a second time. I got up and reached for Karen's hand to pull her up. We brushed the damp grass off our jeans, and then Karen skipped away. She disappeared into the night briefly and then reappeared in the light on her front porch.

I'm going to like having Karen right next door, I thought, *and I know she'll be my friend for a long time. That much is sure.*

Then I remembered Miss Mendoza's letter, which I had stuck into my back pocket. I pulled it from my pocket and carefully peeled open the envelope. I sat on the steps and read by porchlight:

> *Mi'jita, you're a good dancer with an awesome stretch. You've promised to stretch more into ballet, so I will stretch myself and move to Des Plaines. Why not? My dad's getting married after all. And you're there. Clara has invited me to live with her—two gals on the loose. Also, I could drop by often to taste your mother's cooking! Maybe your father could help me find a good used car. Tell him to keep his eyes open for a red convertible! With kisses, Gloria*

"Please move here soon," I whispered. Then Mom called me to come inside. I stood, pirouetted, and danced up the steps and through the front door.

Sunday was so busy that I didn't have much time to worry about Rascal. We got an early start, and Mom decorated my bedroom—the curtains were frilly and my bedspread pink as a thumb. She helped tidy up my chest of drawers and build a shelf for my stuffed animals. Together we put my trunk under the window that faced Karen's house. Then she marked my height on the closet door.

"There," she said. "You're this tall. My little *princesa* is growing up!"

I examined the pencil marking. In six months I will be a little taller, or maybe even a lot taller. I'll just have to wait and see.

Two of Dad's friends helped take out an old refrigerator and move in a new one. Then they moved more furniture up to the second floor.

"Don't hurt yourself, Dad," I yelled from the bottom of the stairs.

"Too late," he groaned. "I think I hurt my pitching arm."

By noon our house was in pretty good order. Mom was so organized that she even had time to make a cake. She no doubt wanted to fill our new home not only with new furniture but also with the smells of baking.

Mom and I drove back and forth to the hardware store for this and that. Early in the afternoon, Dad yelled from the garage, "Marisol, look in the phone book for a pizza delivery."

"You got it, Dad!"

I had been raking leaves and then scattering the leaves again by jumping into the pile. It was fun at first, but without Karen it was just, well, OK. So the thought of pizza made my stomach rumble.

"Let's get a large pepperoni," Dad suggested. He was wearing his baseball mitt instead of work gloves.

"Dad," I asked, "were you good at baseball?"

"The best," he answered with a growl. He shrugged his shoulders. "Well, maybe not the best, but I tried hard." He told me his story. The summer his father bought their first house, Dad was eleven and playing second base on a team that was in next-to-last place. Still, Dad begged his father to let him stay with his grandparents so he could keep playing for his team. But his father wouldn't have it. Dad was needed to help fix up the new house.

"Kind of like me, huh?" I said. "You know, moving away from my dance studio and classes."

"Yeah, mi'ja," he answered softly. "Just like you."

"But you didn't lose a cat like I did," I said. I immediately wished I could call back those words. I had no urge to make Dad feel bad.

"No, but I did lose my dog," Dad confessed sadly.

I didn't feel too good when he told me that his father gave his dog away because no pets were allowed in his new house. I felt sort of like a brat. Rascal had run away. My dad would never give my pet away.

"Enough about pets. And we'll find Rascal," Dad said. "But let's call for that pizza now."

I ran inside and ordered the pizza, along with a salad for three. Then I turned the yellow pages from P for pizza to D for dance. There were no new dance studios listed since the last time I had looked. Would there be some place close by where Miss Mendoza could open her Des Plaines studio? I sighed and went outside to finish raking up the leaves.

Late in the afternoon, Mom came out to the back porch, where Dad and I were staining some woodwork, and announced, "Hector, I left the Mexican planter at the apartment."

The planter had been a gift from her grandmother. Mom's favorite plant grew in it.

"I'll go get it," Dad said wearily. He had been up the earliest of all of us, doing things around the house while I was still in bed.

"No, let me," Mom countered. "I'll pick up a dozen *tamales* from Rosa's." Rosa's is my favorite Mexican restaurant. "You just make some rice. And chop up jalapeños and tomatoes for salsa." To me she said,

"Marisol, why don't you come along so you can look for a certain missing cat." She raised her eyebrows, and then she went inside to get her purse and the car keys.

When we turned onto our old street, I pressed my face to the window. It seemed like I had been gone a long time, but it had only been one day, a few hours, and some minutes.

It was nearly dark. I half expected to see Victor kicking his soccer ball against his garage door, but there was no one on the street.

"You wait here. Then we'll look for Rascal together," Mom said. She got out of the van and disappeared behind the building.

I listened to the engine tick as it cooled. I made out music from far away and the screech of tires at the intersection. Down the street a porch light had gone on and a mother was yelling in Spanish, "Victor, come in now."

This place still felt like home. I got out of the van and looked up. I noticed that Mr. Mendoza's lights were on. He was probably sitting in that big old recliner of his and reading the newspaper. I wondered if Miss Mendoza was sitting there with him.

"Look at them," I whispered to myself as my attention settled on my old bedroom. The stars on my ceiling had caught my eye. They were beautiful, glowing in the very last of the evening light. Suddenly, I had to agree with my parents about being a lucky girl. I *am* lucky. Even though I am losing a lot by moving to Des Plaines, I still have so much. I have my parents. I have a new friend. I am still a dancer. And now I have the promise of Miss Mendoza as my teacher. Still, I wished that I could climb through that window and peel off each and every star.

"But I can't do that," I whispered to myself. The stars will have to be for the next girl who moves in and calls that bedroom her special place. I pictured a girl like me with her elbows on the windowsill, looking down onto the street.

Meow, I heard in the dark. *Meow, meow.*

"Rascal!" I called and felt his hard head rub against my ankle. I scooped him up, hugged him, and scolded, "You naughty, naughty kitty." His cat motor was running, and his nose was poking around my throat.

"I love you, you naughty boy," I cooed.

Rascal meowed.

I had just put Rascal gently in the van when I saw Mom struggling with the planter.

"Let me help," I offered. I picked up one end—it was heavy, all right—and we carried it around to the back of the van.

"Thanks, mi'ja," she said after we placed the planter in the back. "Oh, is that Rascal?"

I didn't have to answer. Rascal meowed for himself.

"You rascal," Mom scolded and leaned in to scratch the scruff of his neck.

Rascal meowed again and hopped over the seat. His tail stood up like a car antenna. He even climbed into his carrier, ready for a ride with his people to his new home.

Mom and I got into the van. It was almost totally dark now, and I liked it that way. As Mom put the van into gear and pulled from the curb, I gazed up one last time to my bedroom. I saw the stars on my ceiling, still glowing and waiting to shine on the next dancing girl.

True Stories

Meet four American girls who,
like Marisol, were born to dance.
They may do different types of dance,
but they've all learned the same thing—
to be your best, put your whole heart,
mind, and soul into whatever
you're striving for.

Annie has been dancing as long as she's been walking. She started taking modern dance lessons when she was only five years old and has been hard at it ever since.

Annie's in dance classes four days a week, and she spends more than fifteen hours each week dancing. Not only is practice fun, but all that work pays off when she goes onstage. Annie usually performs four times a year, and she's had stage fright only once—the very first time she performed on a stage. "Performing is fun, and working hard makes me feel good about what I do," says Annie.

Modern dance is Annie's real love, but this summer she's taking ballet for the first time. "My teacher said that if I want to be a dancer, I need to know other types of dance, too. I'm nervous, but excited."

Sisters Laura and Anna started taking ballet lessons together six years ago and still dance together today. Laura, who is a year older than Anna, likes it that they can practice together at home as well as in the studio. Anna agrees: "And if one of us has a problem, the other can usually help."

Anna and Laura practice together at the barre.

They've performed in *The Nutcracker* as well as in original ballets their academy has staged. Both sisters love performing and have performed as mice, angels, rats, soldiers, puppets, and toys.

Laura and Anna started wearing *pointe* shoes—ballet shoes with hard toes—only after they turned ten, which is the earliest girls can start on pointe. "Toe shoes hurt at first, but not enough to stop dancing," says Laura. Like all ballerinas before her, she's learned to take a deep breath and start dancing—just for the love of it.

For Alinne, being part of a Mexican *baile folklórico*, or folk dance, troupe is a reminder of home. Alinne is from Mexico City, and when she and her mother saw a ballet folklórico performance at a Mexican festival in Wisconsin, they asked to join the troupe. Now they practice every weekend. The more advanced dancers of the group help the younger and newer dancers. Alinne, who's twelve, is one of the youngest and newest members in her troupe, so she has many teachers!

Alinne, who also sings rap and plays basketball, is learning dances from Mexico's many regions, such as Veracruz and Jalisco. Each region has its own traditional costume, so Alinne gets to wear many styles of skirts. Each one is different— but still a warm reminder of home.

A folklórico dancer's most prized possessions are her skirts.

Meet the Author

Gary Soto loves watching dance from a distance, although he will occasionally get onto the dance floor in his 1970s disco suit. He is known to do the splits—sort of. He lives and writes in Berkeley, California.

Glossary of Spanish Words

adios *(ah-dee-OHS)*—good-bye

amiguitos *(ah-mee-GWEE-tohs)*—little friends

asco! *(ah-SKO)*—yuck!

buenas tardes *(BWEH-nahs TAR-dehs)*—good afternoon

burrito *(bur-REE-to)*—a flour tortilla rolled or folded around a filling

cacerolita *(cah-cer-o-LEE-tah)*—small pan

chihuahua *(chee-WAH-wah)*—an exclamation, such as "oh, wow!"

Cielito Lindo *(cee-el-EE-toh LEEN-doh)*—song title, meaning "lovely little heaven"

claro qué sí *(KLAH-ro kay see)*—of course, certainly

danzantes *(dahn-ZAHN-tes)*—dancers

El Caimán *(el ki-MAHN)*—Mexican folk dance about an alligator

El Saus y la Palma *(el sows ee lah PAHL-mah)*—Mexican folk dance about "the willow tree and the palm tree"

enchilada *(en-chee-LAH-dah)*—rolled, filled tortilla baked in a chili sauce

folklórico *(fohlk-LOH-ree-koh)*—folk or folkloric

gracias *(GRAH-see-ahs)*—thank you

jalapeño *(hah-lah-PAIN-yo)*—a type of chili pepper

Jalisco *(hah-LEES-koh)*—a region of Mexico

Jarabe Tapatío *(hah-RAH-bay tah-pah-TEE-oh)*—the Mexican national folk dance

Los Viejitos *(lohs vee-eh-EE-tohs)*—Mexican folk dance about "little old men"

maestra *(mah-EE-strah)*—a title referring to a female teacher

maraca *(mah-RAH-ka)*—a rattle made from a gourd

mejor *(may-HOHR)*—better

mi (mis) *(mee, mees)*—my (plural)

mi'ja *(MEE-hah)*—an endearment, meaning "my daughter"

mi'jita *(mee-HEE-tah)*—an endearment, meaning "my little daughter"

mil *(meel)*—one thousand

molcajete *(mohl-kah-HEH-teh)*—a stone grinding bowl

muy malo *(mwee MAH-lo)*—very bad

novia *(NOH-vee-ah)*—girlfriend

papi *(pah-PEE)*—dad, daddy, or papa

por favor *(pohr fah-VOHR)*—please

princesa *(preen-CHESS-ah)*—princess

raspada *(rah-SPAH-dah)*—snowcone or Popsicle

refritos *(reh-FREE-tohs)*—refried beans

salsa *(SAHL-sah)*—sauce

señorita *(sehn-yohr-EE-tah)*—title meaning "miss"

tamales *(tah-MAH-les)*—spicy meat surrounded by
   cornmeal dough and cooked in a cornhusk wrapping

tortilla *(tor-TEE-yah)*—a kind of flat, round bread made
   of corn or wheat

travieso *(trah-vee-EH-soh)*—troublemaker

ven *(ven)*—come on, come here

ver *(vehr)*—to see

Veracruz *(veh-rah-CROOZ)*—a region of Mexico

French & Ballet Words

barre *(bar)*—wooden bar along a wall or mirror that
   ballet dancers use in practice

battement frappé *(baht-mehnt frah-pay)*—leg and foot exercise that strengthens the muscles

bonjour *(bohn-zhoor)*—hello

chaînes *(shen)*—series of turns in rapid succession

développé *(day-vel-oh-pay)*—movement in which the leg unfolds gradually

echappé *(eh-shah-pay)*—legs move from closed position (legs together) to open (legs apart)

jeté *(zheh-tay)*—jump

mademoiselle *(mahd-mwah-zel)*—title meaning "miss"

merci *(mehr-see)*—thank you

mes petites *(may peh-teet)*—endearment, "my little ones"

pas de chat *(pah deh shah)*—stepping like a cat; leg positions in the air may vary

plié *(plee-ay)*—bend

pointe *(pwahnt)*—point, also hard-toe ballet shoes

relevé *(reh-leh-vay)*—raise

rond de jambe *(rohn deh zhamb)*—a circular leg motion

très bien *(tray byen)*—very good